NAVIGATING
— THE —
WILDERNESS
WITHIN

The Journey from Fear to Freedom

SUZANNE HANNA

Soul Spark Publishing™
An imprint of Soul Spark Enterprises
soulsparkpublishing.com

This is a work of nonfiction. Nevertheless, some names, identifying details, or characteristics of individuals have been changed. Additionally, certain people who have been listed are composites of a number of individuals and their experiences.

This publication is designed to provide accurate and authoritative information in regard to the subject matter covered. It is sold with the understanding that neither the author nor the publisher is engaged in rendering legal, investment, accounting, medical, or other professional services. While the publisher and author have used their best efforts in preparing this book, they make no representations or warranties with respect to the accuracy or completeness of the contents of this book and specifically disclaim any implied warranties of merchantability or fitness for a particular purpose. No warranty may be created or extended by sales representatives or written sales materials. The advice and strategies contained herein may not be suitable for your situation. You should consult with a professional when appropriate. Neither the publisher nor the author shall be liable for any loss of profit or any other commercial damages, including but not limited to special, incidental, consequential, personal, or other damages.

Navigating The Wilderness Within: The Journey From Fear to Freedom, First edition 2025
ISBN 978-1-964445-18-2 (paperback) 978-1-964445-20-5 (ebook) 978-1-964445-19-9 (hardcover)
Map and Icon art by Gloria Owens, Fish Cat Design
Cover and interior image sourced on Adobe Stock

NAVIGATING
THE
WILDERNESS
WITHIN

Soul Spark
PUBLISHING

DEDICATION

To Grace, the closest I have ever come to holding God in the flesh.
And to my Mother, for believing in me.

TABLE OF CONTENTS

PREFACE

Dear Fellow Journeyer,

Welcome to the opening pages of a journey, one that transcends the boundaries of the written word and invites you to embark on a transformative exploration of your own internal wilderness.

As you turn these pages, consider them not just as words on paper but as guideposts, leading you toward a deeper understanding of yourself and the limitless possibilities that lie within. May this offering be a faithful companion on your quest for self-discovery, inner freedom, and wholehearted living.

In these chapters, we'll navigate the complexities of the human experience together. We'll explore the pathways of your thoughts, the depths of your emotions, and the expansiveness of your desires. This is a space for reflection, growth, and the steadfast belief that every person has the innate capacity to evolve and thrive.

Whether you find yourself at a painful crossroads, yearning for a deeper connection with yourself, or feeling the pull to rise into the truth of who you really are, know that you are not alone; I am walking with you. This pilgrimage is a shared journey, one of introspection, upheavals, and the soul-shifting power that comes when you are courageous enough to take the first step upon a trail that leads deep into uncharted territory.

Scattered throughout, you'll also find personal messages from me, short notes written just for you. Think of them as moments where we meet on the path, a pause to connect heart-to-heart. These letters are my way of reaching across the distance to stand beside you, to be a comforting voice when you need it most.

So, as you begin this odyssey of inner awakening, I encourage you to approach it with an open heart and a curious mind. Curl up with a warm cup of tea, wrap yourself in a soft blanket, and keep a journal nearby. Let this book take you deep into yourself, into the parts that have been waiting to be seen, heard, and remembered. My prayer is that you allow whatever needs to arise to come forward, without resistance or judgment. Some moments may be tender, unexpected, or deeply stirring, a box of tissues may be handy.

May this experience spark a deeper knowing of who you were created to be in this lifetime. May you find the courage to embrace change, the fortitude to face the trials along the trail, and the wisdom to open the door to what is waiting for you. It is time to give yourself permission to walk into the intricate landscape that is you; both shadow and light.

In writing this book, I cracked open in new and unexpected ways. I also experienced greater freedom and joy. I hope it does the same for you.

Let the journey begin.

A RITE OF PASSAGE

Within the expansive, uncharted landscape of the human spirit lies an untamed wilderness, an endless terrain of solitude, struggle, and ultimate transformation. Every soul, at some point, must venture into this shadowed territory, not to battle external forces, but to confront the deepest, most hidden parts of themselves.

Throughout history, such journeys have been more than trials of endurance, they are sacred rites of passage, initiations through which we reclaim our essence. This is not merely a test, but a calling: to shed illusion, to stand bare and unguarded before the truth that lives beneath our roles, defenses, and conditioning, and to activate the untapped power that has always dwelled within us.

Jesus' Desert Walk

In a quiet stretch of sun-scorched desert, Jesus embarked on a 40-day and 40-night quest—a journey not just of physical endurance but of spiritual awakening. Alone with the endless dunes, He faced temptations, doubts, and the hollow hush of isolation. The desert was both His battleground and His sanctuary, where each grain of sand carried secrets of resilience and purpose. In that crucible of silence, He unearthed the strength to embrace His destiny, transforming the wilderness into a source of divine inspiration.

Tubman's Road to Liberation

Through the tangled thickets of the Eastern Woodlands and beneath the vast canopy of the evening sky, Harriet Tubman walked her wilderness, one of danger, defiance, and destiny. Born into bondage, she had known the cold grip of shackles, but the call of freedom rang louder. Guided by the North Star and an unshakable faith, she carved a path to liberation, not only for herself, but for countless others. Her wilderness was more than the perilous ground she crossed; it was the inner terrain where fear collided with fierce conviction. Every journey back into the South was a brush with death, yet she did not falter. She listened, not to doubt, but to the still, unwavering voice within, the one that told her she was meant for something greater.

Gandhi's Path of Nonviolence

In a land of clashing colors and ceaseless turmoil, Gandhi's heart was a map of unyielding compassion and steadfast conviction. His own internal wilderness was marked by moments of deep reflection, where the cries of pain met the quiet call of hope. Through long walks, meditations, and acts of simple, deliberate kindness, he cultivated a garden of nonviolence within, even amid the tumult of a national revolution. This personal uprising, born of solitude and self-inquiry, became the beacon of his lifelong quest to transform a nation, proving that the deepest battles are often waged within the self.

Mandela's March Toward Freedom

Far across the ocean, in the harrowing reality of apartheid, behind cold, immovable prison walls, Nelson Mandela embarked on his own inner pilgrimage. The years of confinement were not merely a physical imprisonment but a call to explore the depths of his spirit. Amidst despair, Mandela nurtured an inner revolution, a determination that grew with every long, lonely day. His mind wandered through corridors of past memories and future dreams, eventually lighting a spark that would guide not only his own passage to freedom but inspire a country to break its chains. His internal journey was a testament to the transcendent power of resilience and forgiveness.

A Universal Call to Wander

As we trace the footsteps of some of history's most courageous figures—Jesus, Tubman, Gandhi, Mandela—a deeper truth emerges: we are all called to traverse our own internal wilderness. Just as their journeys tested their spirits and reshaped their destinies, so too must each of us confront the rugged wild within. These visionary leaders remind us that self-exploration is not reserved for the chosen few but is a fundamental rite of passage in the human experience, an essential step in our evolution.

The internal wilderness is the very heart of the hero's journey, where the call to adventure is not an external summons but an inner reckoning. In its harsh beauty, every challenge becomes a catalyst for growth, urging us to step forward with courage and determination. The sacred solitude of our inner realm is not an escape but an invitation to face ourselves, to wrestle with our fears, and ultimately to surpass the limits of who we once were.

In every quiet moment of reflection, every shadowed fear, and every glimmer of hope, our souls are gently urging us forward. We are no different from those who have come before; our internal battles and victories are the silent markers of our strength. Like the heroes of myth and legend, we must descend into the unknown, confront our shadows, and emerge transformed. Whether in moments of heartbreak or in the light of newfound understanding, the wilderness asks us to embrace our vulnerabilities and rise stronger.

The only way to live a meaningful, conscious life is to truly understand ourselves— and that depth of self-awareness can only be forged in the dark. It's through these solitary journeys that we awaken the power of introspection, turning life's trials into stepping stones toward a more enlightened existence. As we navigate our own inner wilderness, we become part of a shared human story, a collective odyssey toward strength, wisdom, and untapped potential.

HOW TO USE THIS BOOK

This book is a collection of reflections from both my life and the journey that transformed it—stories etched into my spirit by the wind, mountains, and the endless trails beneath my feet. More than that, it's an offering to help you find your own way forward, not by giving answers, but by reminding you that you already carry them within.

What matters most isn't the miles I walked, but the wisdom gathered along the way. My focus is less on what happened and more on how it shaped me, how it opened a deeper understanding of myself, of life, and of the unfolding path you, too, are walking. I offer my story in the hope that it may serve your own healing.

Here, I'll reveal the insights that shook me, challenged me, and ultimately set me free. I'll walk with you through the shadows, the doubt, and the parts of yourself you may have tried to hide. Step by step, you'll enter the vast landscape of your own heart and soul. You won't only read about my journey, you'll be invited to explore your own. With this guidebook close at hand, you can trace the places where fear, longing, and hidden truths are calling you toward a more embodied, meaningful way of living.

This quest, yours and mine, is about courage. About learning to trust yourself. About stepping into the unknown, even when fear tells you to turn back. It's about finding your way home to your truth, and to that wilder, more wondrous life waiting just beyond the walls of everything you were told to be.

So as you move through these pages, let these words walk beside you, challenge you, encourage you, and remind you that even in your most uncertain moments, you have never been truly alone.

TRAIL WISDOM

Guideposts for the journey

Throughout this book, you'll encounter what I call *Trail Wisdom*—guideposts for your own inner pilgrimage. These aren't insights pulled from theory or textbooks, but truths born of lived experience. From blisters and breakdowns to beauty and silence, they are the revelations the trail offered when I finally had no choice but to listen.

Each one is a small, potent offering, a compass for the soul. Think of them as markers inviting you to pause, reflect, and surrender to the initiatory fire calling you forward. My journey was never just about the terrain I hiked; it was about how it broke me open, remade me, and unearthed messages I now offer to you.

The trail is more than a passage. It is a teacher, calling you toward growth, urging you into the unknown with an open heart, and reminding you to trust the quiet voice within even when the map disappears.

The healing it offers isn't found at some final destination. It lives in the journey itself. With each step, you release what no longer serves, reclaim your voice, and gather back the parts of yourself you once abandoned.

Trail Wisdom is a living inheritance, carried by those who walked this path long ago and kept alive by those who journey beside you now. Even in solitude, you follow echoes—footprints pressed into the earth, stories etched into bark and stone. Their resilience, surrender, and endurance light the way forward.

Like a torch, it's passed from hand to hand. Each traveler adds to its glow. You are both student and steward of the path, learning from your own steps, drawing strength from those who persevered before you, and carrying the responsibility to share your own hard-earned lessons with those who will one day follow.

Walking this sacred way is not just about forward motion; it's about presence. It reminds you that every voyage, whether through the actual wilderness or the mystery of life itself, isn't about arriving. It's about how you travel. Endurance lives not only in pushing forward, but in knowing when to pause, when to listen, and when to extend a hand to someone who needs it.

Each step, each insight, becomes part of a greater story, one that connects past, present, and future seekers. The message of the trail continues, an unbroken thread woven through time, calling you to walk with courage, to learn with humility, and to share with a compassionate heart.

So when the road ahead feels uncertain, when self-doubt rises and you begin to wonder if you're lost, remember this:

Keep going. The path will reveal itself as you walk.

GUIDED VISUALIZATIONS

Portals to inner vision and truth

This book isn't just meant to be read, it's meant to be *lived*. Each section marks a turning point on the evolutionary path. That's why, at the beginning of each chapter, you'll find a guided visualization, an intentional pause, an opportunity to shift from thinking into feeling.

Words can point the way, but real change happens in direct experience—through felt sense, imagery, and embodiment. These visualizations aren't exercises; they are sacred encounters, designed to carry you beyond the surface of thought and into the places within you that have long awaited your attention.

In the liminal space between breath and imagination, you may meet forgotten parts of yourself. You may hear the faint longings of your spirit, see visions rising from the depths, or feel messages awaken in your bones. Trust what comes. There is no wrong way to walk this path.

Everything here is meant to draw you more fully into yourself.

THE MAP

Trailmarkers for the Journey

On the following page, you'll find a map—not of a place, but of a passage. It's a living blueprint, carved from my own footsteps and drawn from the choices I've made and the challenges I've faced. It traces the contours of the Hero's Journey, that ancient call to leave the known behind and venture into the unknown.

Here, the wilderness we walk is the wilderness within.

Each step is more than a moment in time; it is an unearthing, a deep excavation of self. This is not only the story of my path. It is an invitation to step fully into yours, a hand extended across the chasm of fear and uncertainty, saying: *Come. There is a way through. I will walk with you.*

Maps do not dictate your direction, but they offer orientation when the way grows dark. They remind you that others have traveled this terrain—that you, too, can survive the seasons of loss, confusion, fear, and healing. A map gives form to mystery, not to confine it, but to help you stay awake inside it.

You may recognize yourself in its stages.
You may find your own footsteps mirrored here.
Or you may blaze an entirely new trail.

Remember this: the map is never the destination—*you are.*
Let it be an ally, a comfort, and a witness to your unfolding. It may point the way, but its deeper gift is the reminder that transformation happens in the spaces between guideposts, not in the arrival, but in the walking itself.

Above all, trust the wilderness inside you.
It knows the way home.

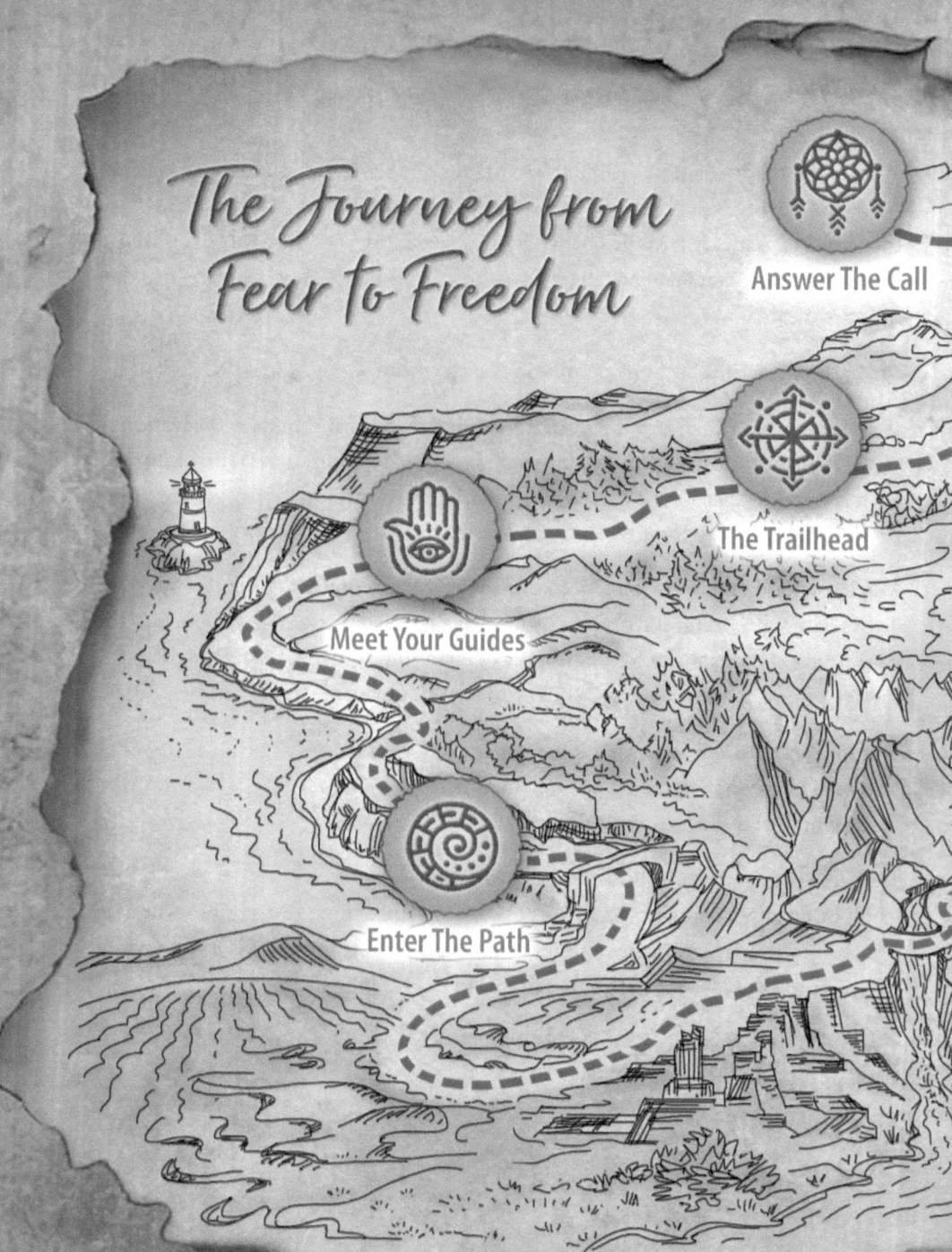

The Wilderness

New Life

Path To Freedom

Embodying The Light

es & Trials

Map art by Gloria Owens, Fish Cat Design

THE GUIDED JOURNAL

An Invitation to Go Deeper

This book is more than a story; it is a truth wrapped in love. As you read, you may recognize fragments of your own life woven through these experiences. This is no accident. The wilderness inside you is listening.

To receive what's here is not only to turn the pages, but to let the words sink in, to awaken what's been buried, and to follow the call into the wild, uncharted realm of your soul.

That is why I created the *Navigating the Wilderness Within* guided journal. Inside, you'll find reflections, prompts, and open space for inquiry—tools to help you listen inward and notice what is rising. You can move through it alongside each chapter or return to it whenever the moment calls.

The only way through is the way you choose.

INTRODUCTION

I never imagined a walk in the woods would change the course of my life. But it did. This wasn't a gentle stroll through sun-dappled forests with birds serenading my every step. No. this was something entirely different—a raw, unrelenting plunge into the mysterious depths of my own being.

I had set out on a 1,000-mile trek across the wide and wild expanse of the United States with my golden retriever, Grace. At the time, I didn't fully understand what I was stepping into. I only knew that I was exhausted, tired of running from my own reflection, from fear, and a life that felt too confining for the person I longed to become. Deep down, I craved disruption. Something radical enough to wake me up.

And wake me it did.

What I didn't anticipate was how quickly the real wilderness would reveal itself, and it wasn't in the rugged mountains or the misted forests. The true frontier lay within, an unexplored realm teeming with shadows I had spent a lifetime avoiding. It was messy and unpredictable, far more challenging than any trail beneath my feet.

One night, early in the journey, somewhere deep in the woods of Virginia, the rain came down so hard it felt like the sky had cracked open. My backpack was soaked. Grace was curled into a damp ball beside me. I sat there in the dark—shivering, hungry, and questioning every life decision that had led me to this moment. No shelter, no dry socks, no cell service. Just me, my wet dog, and the realization that I had voluntarily signed up for this.

There were countless moments like that, when I stumbled, cried, and screamed into the void, certain I wouldn't make it through. The weight of my emotions was unbearable at times. My thoughts threatened to consume me. Every tender part I carried, every choice I had made, every relationship that had shaped or shattered me, resurfaced somewhere along the trail, asking to be seen.

I didn't "find" myself in the wilderness, not in the poetic, paradoxical way people often describe it. I unraveled—viscerally, painstakingly, and sometimes agonizingly. I lost myself completely. My identity, my defenses, the stories I had clung to—one by one, they fell away, until only the most essential part of me remained. The part that had nothing to prove.

The wilderness within doesn't gently ask you to stop running, it demands it. It doesn't offer polite invitations to sit with discomfort, it drops you to your knees. It forces you to face the parts of yourself you've locked inside, the ones you'd rather not acknowledge. It dismantles the illusions you hold on to and fractures the walls you thought would keep you safe.

At first, it feels like chaos. You're disoriented, untethered, unsure of who you are without the stories you've told yourself. But as the dust begins to settle, you start to see clearly—yourself, your life, and your brilliance waiting underneath it all.

To enter this realm is to confront what it means to be fully human. It means peeling back the layers of conditioning and expectation to reveal the beating heart of your existence. It requires courage, because here, there are no clear paths, no guarantees of safety. Only a deep inner knowing that this—*this*—is what you were made for.

And something miraculous begins to happen. As you learn to navigate your own inner landscape, a portal opens, one that leads to liberation.

You slow down. You listen differently. You start to trust the instincts you once silenced in the name of being good, accepted, and safe. You begin to hear your voice again, not the one you were taught to use, but the one that rises from deep within, the one you forgot was ever there.

Eventually, we all find ourselves in the wilderness. Maybe not on a literal trail, but in the depths of our own unraveling, in the moment when life no longer fits and the old ways no longer work. And in that place, if you are willing to stay, you begin to reclaim yourself.

True freedom doesn't come from achievement, approval, or security. It comes from knowing who you are at your core and choosing to live in alignment with that truth, no matter how the world may judge you. It is the release of fear and obligation. And it is the freedom to create, love, risk, and dream.

The journey isn't easy, but it is a necessary one. That's why I wrote this book, not because I have all the answers, but because I know what it means to walk through the dark without a compass and emerge, not unscathed, but whole. My story is simply one path through the wild.

My hope is that these words found you at just the right time. Maybe you're standing at the edge of your own wilderness, wondering if you have the courage to step in. If so, know this: the journey will break you, yes—but it will also set you free.

This path is not about arriving at some final destination. There is no finish line where everything suddenly becomes resolved. This journey is an evolution, a steady return to the person you were always meant to be. With every step, you will shed old layers, old identities, old fears. You will grow, shift, and expand in ways you cannot yet imagine.

So if you feel the pull, if something inside you comes alive at the thought of stepping into the unknown, trust it. Because the wilderness does not call those who are meant to stay the same. It always calls those who are ready to rise.

THE CATALYST

We all have catalysts that send us into the wilderness, life-altering events that insist you shed your old skin and step into something new, something unseen, something essential.

Catalysts take many forms—heartbreak, loss, perceived failure, betrayal, illness, or unexpected change. Sometimes they arrive as a single, eye-opening realization that alters the way you see yourself and the world around you. They may come wrapped in pain or arrive through conscious choice, feeling like destruction in the moment, but in truth, they are creation in disguise.

For me, the catalyst was a relationship that shattered every illusion I had about love and left me feeling more lost and alone than ever before.

It didn't come out of nowhere, I had a long-standing pattern of choosing men who weren't fully available, emotionally, spiritually, physically, or sometimes even geographically. I told myself that with enough love and patience, I could "fix" them. I confused overgiving with intimacy and self-sacrifice for connection. What I called commitment slowly eroded into self-abandonment.

So, true to form, I began shrinking to meet his expectations, staying quiet to avoid conflict, and tolerating judgment and emotional distance as if that were love. I craved affection and treated every half-hearted text or distracted compliment like it was a grand romantic gesture. Over time, I became an expert in excuses: *He's just going through a lot... he's scared of how deep this connection is... Mercury is in retrograde.* But beneath it all was a deeper truth I struggled to admit: I wasn't just afraid of losing him.

I was afraid of facing another failure.
Another heartbreak.
Another "love" slipping through my fingers as I approached forty.

One morning, I lay motionless in his bed, my body heavy, as if bound by invisible chains. The air felt oppressive, making even the smallest movement feel impossible. My eyes drifted to the ceiling, where hairline cracks splintered through the paint. I traced their jagged paths, as if they might explain how I had ended up here—empty, frozen, on the edge of something I couldn't yet name.

Beside me, there was a steady rhythm of breathing, not his, but our dog's. The yellow lab I had brought home nearly three years earlier, a birthday gift meant to soften his heart. But it hadn't. Instead, this gentle creature became my refuge, the only warmth in a space that had grown unbearably cold.

I reached for him, running my fingers through his soft fur, grounding myself in the rise and fall of his breath. And I knew then: to leave this loyal pup would break my heart, just as surely as staying with this man would break my spirit.

But beneath that heartbreak, something older, deeper, and truer was beginning to rise, an awareness that could no longer be silenced. I had reached a threshold, a breaking point I'd spent months, maybe even years, pretending wasn't coming. It didn't crash in all at once. It crept in slowly, through small, insidious patterns: the way I waited for my boyfriend's approval before making even the simplest decisions—what to wear, what to eat. The way I tiptoed around his moods, always careful not to trigger another wave of silence or criticism. The way I dismissed my own needs just to keep him comfortable. Still, I kept convincing myself it would get better. That I just needed to try harder, be more patient, be less...*me.*

But the truth was, I had been disappearing for a long time. Quietly erasing parts of myself to keep the peace, to feel wanted, to avoid rocking the boat. The pain had built to a point where pushing it aside was no longer possible. If I didn't leave, I would vanish completely.

I forced myself to move, peeling back the covers and stepping onto the cold wooden floor. My legs felt unsteady, but I made it to the bathroom, gripping the edges of the cool porcelain sink as I lifted my eyes to the mirror. The woman staring back at me was unrecognizable. Her face was drawn, her eyes empty. No light, no fire, just the reflection of a life that had drained her of everything she once was.

Tears streamed down her cheeks, washing away years of denial, excuses, and fear. And beneath the grief, something long buried began to emerge. A pulse of courage, faint but steady, whispering: *You are still here. You are still breathing. You are still capable of choosing yourself.*

But knowing this—deeply, undeniably knowing it—was not enough. Because now, I had to speak it. I had to say the words that would expose what I'd tried so hard not to admit—the truth that had been building quietly inside me, even as I kept pretending everything was fine. Speaking them would send ripples through the life I had built, no matter how broken it already was.

I stood there for a moment, heart pounding, torn between the safety of silence and the cost of truth. Then I walked back into the bedroom, where he was getting dressed for work.

"I can't do this anymore."

His eyes darkened, confusion flashing into something sharper. "What are you saying?" I swallowed, holding back tears. "I'm leaving. This isn't working anymore, not for either of us."

Silence.

And then, just as I expected, came the resistance.
The guilt about the dog.
The anger disguised as love.
The dismissal of my words.
The attempts to pull me back into the safety of the known.

He looked at me and said, dismissively, "You don't really want that."

His words landed like anchors, each one reaching for the part of me that still doubted. Every sentence was a tether, an invisible thread meant to pull me back into the dysfunction I was trying to escape. I had heard them all before. Hell, I had even said them to myself in my darkest moments, convincing myself to hold on just a little longer. That it would get better, that I was asking for too much, that I was just restless, that love was hard, that the grass wasn't always greener.

But something in me had shifted. I had stood at this crossroads before and turned back, allowing the fear of the unknown to pull me into complacency. I had swallowed my voice to prevent another argument. I had buried my needs beneath guilt. I had stayed when every fiber of my being had begged me to run.

Not this time.

I met his gaze, steady now. No longer searching for permission. No longer waiting for validation. It was one of the hardest and most liberating conversations I had ever had.

What I learned that day is this: Hard conversations have a way of stripping everything down to the truth. They expose what's real beneath the stories you tell yourself. They shine a light on what is and isn't working. And they demand honesty, not just with the other person, but with your own heart.

Maybe you've been there. Maybe you're there now. Delaying the reckoning, convincing yourself that silence is safer. That if you ignore the fractures, they might heal on their own. But avoidance doesn't heal; it only prolongs the inevitable. Eventually, you're left standing in the rubble of all that's been left unsaid. And that's when you finally see it: hard conversations don't end things. They reveal them.

They uncover the brokenness you've ignored. They show you where understanding has eroded, where your needs have gone unmet for far too long. What is unearthed in these moments either moves you toward healing or toward an ending. There is no middle ground. Only the slow erosion of self through withholding, compromise, and the denial of your own truth.

And in facing what is revealed, you'll discover something else: you cannot attach yourself to how the other person receives your words. You are not responsible for their reactions, only for your commitment to transparency. Hard conversations are not about control, persuasion, manipulation, or winning. They are about standing in integrity, no matter the outcome.

If you face them with honesty and a willingness to grow, they can become the foundation of something stronger. But if you ignore them, if you turn away from the truth they expose, a breakdown is inevitable.

Silence is not protection. It is a slow decay. You may believe that avoiding conflict is the same as keeping love alive. But love built on silence is not love at all. It is fear draped in devotion.

THE EMPTY SPACE

Once I left my relationship, I stepped into an uncharted world. I would often look back at the wreckage and wonder how I had survived it for so long. And yet, a part of me wanted to run back, if only to escape the unbearable emptiness stretching out before me.

There was a constant heaviness in my chest, an eerie stillness in spaces once filled with distractions, conversations, and companionship. My mind fixated on the good times, twisting memories into something more wonderful than they had been. The laughter, the connection, the moments that felt real, those were the ones that lingered, making me question everything. Had I expected too much? Had I thrown away something that could have been salvaged with several years of intensive therapy?

It wasn't the relief I had imagined. It wasn't liberation, it was absence. Like escaping a suffocating room only to find myself in a large, empty space, disoriented and unsteady. I had braced myself for sadness, maybe even anger, but I wasn't prepared for the intense grief, for the way I could miss something that had once caused me so much pain.

I felt vulnerable and stripped to the bone. The new house I had bought felt just as hollow as I did. I drifted through the hallways, unmoored, searching for something solid to hold onto. I had no idea where I was going, only that I couldn't go back.

More than anything, I missed our dog, the one constant, loving presence in my life. His familiar weight against my legs, the peaceful sound of his breathing at night, the way he always seemed to know when I needed comfort. I wanted to go back for him.

But deep down, I knew better. Taking him with me would've been a way of holding on, clinging to a past I was trying desperately to walk away from. Even sharing him, trading days or splitting time, would have kept me tied to someone I needed to let go of. And though it hurt, I knew he was safe. He was loved. And that had to be enough.

Still, the emptiness gnawed at me. I needed something to ground me, to remind me I was still capable of love and still capable of moving forward. So, I made a decision.

I would return to the same breeder where I had gotten our previous dog. Not to replace what I had lost, but to open my heart to a new companion, one who could walk beside me as I stepped into the next chapter of my life.

EYES THAT REMEMBER

I drove to the breeder with a pit in my stomach, my hands tightening around the wheel as I pulled into the gravel lot. I wasn't sure I was ready for this.

The old barn stood just ahead, weathered wood faded to a soft gray, its wide doors open to the late afternoon light. It looked exactly as I remembered, nestled in the stillness of quiet farmland, where golden fields stretched endlessly toward the horizon.

The moment I stepped inside, I was enveloped by a familiar scent, a mix of warm puppy fur and the piercing aroma of disinfectant. Then, chaos erupted. A chorus of barks filled the space, paws skittering against metal crates in a desperate bid for attention. Tiny noses pressed through wire doors. Tails thudded against walls. It was loud, messy and alive. I smiled, and for a moment, I forgot how heavy my heart had been.

The breeder recognized me instantly. She was just as I remembered—soft eyes, silver hair loosely braided down her back, and an energy that radiated calm. There was something grounded and reassuring about her presence.

As I explained my situation, a pang of guilt lodged itself deep in my gut. Was this betrayal? Replacing my dog with another? The thought unsettled me, made me want to run. Sensing my hesitation, she placed a gentle hand on my arm.

"Stay," she said softly, as if she knew I was already halfway gone. "I think I know exactly what you need." Something in her tone, something knowing, made me pause. And so, I stayed.

She slipped into a back room and returned moments later, cradling a small bundle of golden fur.

"She was left behind," she said gently. "Her new owners changed their minds."

She placed the puppy in my arms, a golden retriever with oversized paws and velvety ears. She was impossibly soft, her fur warm beneath my fingers. As she wriggled closer, her long, eager tongue swiped at my chin, her tiny body trembling slightly. She melted into my arms as if she had been waiting for this moment, for someone to choose her.

Then she lifted her head, her deep, chocolate-brown eyes locking onto mine. And I felt it—goosebumps rose on my skin, a spark of recognition. It was as if she could see straight through me, that she understood the burdens I carried, the silent ache I hadn't yet learned how to hold.

We were both lost. Each of us, abandoned in our own way. I cradled her closer, breathing in her warmth, and something inside me softened, something that had been clenched tight for far too long.

In that instant, I knew. Not with logic, not with reason, but with a deep, undeniable certainty that settled into my bones.

I hadn't found her. She had found me.

I thanked the breeder, paid for my puppy, and stepped outside, a new sense of hope and excitement buzzing through my body. The moment I settled this sweet pup into the car, a wave of realization crashed over me, she was mine. Not just to hold or play with, but to care for, protect, and nurture. This tiny, fragile creature needed me. The truth is, we needed each other.

I glanced at her in the backseat through the rearview mirror as I drove. Her oversized paws were splayed for balance, her head wobbling like a dashboard bobblehead with every turn. I smiled, just in time for her to let out a tiny whimper and then hurl all over the seat.

With a sigh, I pulled to the side of the road, reaching for the nearest napkin. As I cleaned her up, she gazed up at me with wide, knowing eyes, as if they held a sacred message I had yet to uncover.

That's when it hit me, I hadn't even given her a name.

I sat there, staring at her, thinking about what I had felt the moment she looked at me. Some things in life arrive unplanned, unexpected. They shake us, shift us, remind us of something we didn't even know we had lost. And yet, they belong to us in a way that reason can't explain. They come from somewhere deeper. From grace itself—unearned, unexplainable, but exactly what we need. I ran my fingers over her soft ears and whispered, "Grace. Your name is Grace."

THE MEDICINE IN THE WILD

My healing journey began with daily walks through a beautiful 1,775-acre nature preserve near my new home. The sprawling forests, open meadows, winding rivers, and hidden wetlands became my refuge, a sanctuary from the buried pain I had carried for so long. There was always a particular kind of calm I could only find in the woods. As a child, I spent countless hours hiking the rugged trails of New Hampshire's White Mountains with my family, riding horses beneath towering oaks, and seeking solace in the wild places where my spirit felt free, where I could breathe, feel, and simply be.

Now, as my life unraveled around me, I found myself drawn to the woods once more, not just to escape, but to listen, heal, and find my way back to myself.

With each step, the weight I'd been carrying began to ease. The scent of earth and pine grounded me. The wind moved gently through the trees, offering quiet reassurance. And the chorus of birds overhead became a kind of living meditation, melodic and soothing.

Slowly, the numbness that had gripped me began to thaw, and with it the pain loosened its hold. The fog that had clouded everything started to lift. And for the first time in what felt like forever, I could finally breathe again.

Grace trotted beside me, her nose twitching at the scent of damp leaves and the musky odor of the woodland's hidden dwellers. She greeted every passing hiker with a curious sniff and an eager wag of her tail, often receiving words of praise and affection in return. But it was the squirrels and chipmunks that truly captivated her, the tiny, darting creatures that zipped through the underbrush and disappeared into the trees. With boundless energy, she sprang into motion, leaping over fallen logs, weaving through tree trunks, and chasing shadows with childlike wonder. She was wild and free, completely in her element.

Each season in the preserve held its own special magic. Winter wrapped the forest in a hush of snow, muffling sound and slowing time. In spring, the land awakened as the rivers swelled with melted ice and the trees stretched toward the sun. By summer, everything pulsed with life—sunlight spilling through the canopy in golden ribbons, birds chirping, bees drifting lazily from bloom to bloom, and the fragrance of wildflowers rising on the breeze. Then came autumn, the most breathtaking of all. The trees exploded in crimson, gold, and fiery amber, setting the world ablaze before surrendering their leaves to the wind.

Despite the serenity the preserve offered, a deep longing still lived inside me, something I couldn't name, only feel. It wasn't just emptiness. It was a void, an unsettling sense that I was watching my own life from a distance, more a witness than a participant. It wasn't the same lost feeling I had known in my relationship, that kind had been stifling. This was something else: more elusive, more disorienting, as if I were drifting, unmoored, between who I was and who I was meant to be.

My daily routines grew monotonous, each day blending into the next. In my work as a psychotherapist, I sat face to face with depression, anxiety, trauma, and abuse. I held space for the pain of others, absorbing their sorrow until it descended into my own body. I loved my work, yet it had become overwhelming and exhausting over the years. Despite my thriving practice, a beautiful office, a full client list, and a schedule packed well beyond forty hours a week, I felt like an imposter. My own life was quietly unraveling and the once-welcoming walls of my office now felt confining, closing in like an invisible cage.

Deep within, a force pulled at me relentlessly. It was an unshakable urge to break away, to step into something radically different, something that might change the direction of my life. But fear held me in place. Fear of financial uncertainty. Fear of stepping into the great unknown. So I gripped tightly to what was familiar, to the safety of predictability, even as my spirit begged for more.

THE TURNING POINT

One afternoon in the nature preserve with Grace, we wandered into a beautiful meadow. The sun hung high in a cloudless sky, bathing everything in luminous light. The air carried the scent of wildflowers—bursts of purple, yellow, and white swaying gently among the tall grasses. I lowered myself to the ground, tilting my face toward the warmth of the sun. For the first time in a long while, I let myself be completely still.

Grace was anything but. She bounded through the fields, her joy so pure it felt like a living prayer. She leapt with unfiltered abandon, light on her feet, as if she'd never carried a single worry. There was something about the way she moved that tugged at me. I yearned for that kind of aliveness, the kind of freedom that runs barefoot, without apology or fear.

Then, out of nowhere, she barreled into me, and we tumbled into the grass. She flopped across my chest, her warm, wiggly body pressing into mine as she let out a deep, contented sigh. Her nose nestled into the crook of my neck, and her paws came to rest softly on my arm. As I lay there, breathless in the presence of her absolute trust, something in me clicked. I knew, without question, what I had to do.

I would leave. I would step away from the life that had grown too tight, too small. I would take time off, travel with Grace, and see the world through her eyes. I would finally face my deepest fear, my fear of being alone.

More than just leaving the old behind, I wanted to immerse myself in the expansive raw beauty of nature. To wander through the towering pines of the North, feel the sun sink behind the red rocks of the West, breathe in the salty air of the Eastern shores, and lose myself in the endless flaxen fields of the South. I wanted to walk the country's untamed trails, every winding path leading me deeper into myself.

I had no idea how I would make it work. My life was a carefully structured machine, a calendar filled to the brim with obligations. But at that moment, it didn't feel like a choice. It felt like survival. My soul wasn't asking for this: *it was demanding it.* And I knew that if I ignored it, I'd slowly wither inside the cage I had built around myself. I had to go. My life depended on it.

A NEW BEGINNING

I ran home, burst through my front door, my heart pounding with possibility. I dug through a forgotten stack of books until my fingers closed around an old gas-station atlas—the kind with creased, oversized pages and the scent of dust and adventure. Spreading it across the floor, I traced my fingers over the winding highways, the majestic mountain ranges, the endless trails stretching from coast to coast. With each turn of the page my excitement grew. I could see it all—the deserts shimmering under the sun, the dense forests sharing their secrets, the rugged mountains imbuing my body with strength. I imagined the earth beneath my feet, the wind in my hair, Grace bounding beside me, joyful and carefree.

Grace had already shown me that healing was possible. At just over a year old, she had become more than a trusted friend. She was a guide, a mirror, a force of nature reminding me that life isn't something to endure, but to embrace. And I had the sense that she had more to teach me, if I could just slow down enough to pay attention.

Almost immediately the voice that masks itself as "reason" tried to veto my dream: What about your job? Your responsibilities? Doubt slithered in like a snake, suffocating my excitement. For a moment, I felt defeated, teetering on the edge of abandoning the idea before it had a chance to fully land in my body.

I called my mother, hoping for reassurance, but the moment I told her, she gasped.

"Are you crazy? You'll end up in a body bag, beheaded by some serial killer in the woods!" I sighed. It wasn't unexpected. My mother lived in fear, she always had. She watched the news religiously, absorbing every horrific story and letting it take hold of her. To her, the world was a terrifying place, full of danger lurking in every shadow. She often spoke in warnings, in worst-case scenarios, in what-ifs that paralyzed rather than prepared. Fear had stolen so much from her. I had watched it tighten its grip over the years, watched her trade adventure for caution, passion for practicality. It wasn't until much later in life that I saw her begin to do the things that she had long kept at bay.

I didn't want that to be my fate. I refused to spend my life locked in a prison of what-ifs, watching the years slip away while I clung to the illusion of safety. I wanted to live, not just exist, not just survive, but truly live.

Most of my friends were supportive, their voices a mix of encouragement and concern. Some called me brave, their words laced with admiration, as if I were embarking on some grand, noble quest. Others weren't so sure. Some called me impulsive, shaking their heads, their worry evident even as they tried to mask it behind polite smiles and questions like, *"Do you even own a backpack?"*

Maybe I was both. Maybe I needed to be. Because I knew, deep in my heart, that nothing would change unless I made it happen. Playing it safe had only ever kept me stuck, and I wasn't willing to do that anymore.

The logistics weren't impossible. I could take four weeks off at a time, breaking my journey into pieces over the next few years. I didn't need to do it all at once, just enough to keep moving, to keep stepping into the unknown.

And I would do it. Because the fire was lit. The dream had taken hold. And if I didn't chase it now, while I still had the courage, I might never find it again.

Just then, as if sensing the change in me, Grace walked over and sat beside me. She looked straight into my eyes, her gaze steady. Slowly, she rested her head on my shoulder, pressing into me with an unmistakable knowing. She could always see straight into my soul, past the doubt, right down into the fire of my heart's longing for change. She blinked once, slow and deliberate. The deal was sealed. We were going.

GUIDED BY GRACE

Before we left, I took a wilderness survival class, eager to prepare for the journey ahead. They drilled into me the dangers of the backcountry, how a twisted ankle miles from help could turn deadly, how the cold could creep in and steal your life before morning, and how the wilderness was indifferent to whether you survived or not.

But when they warned me that Grace could attract predators—coyotes, mountain lions, even bears—I made a decision: we wouldn't camp. The thought of her being seen as prey was unbearable, and the idea of myself in the same vulnerable position was just as unsettling. I also had no intention of sending my mother into a panic-induced sedative spiral. Instead, we would rise with the sun, hike from dawn until dusk, letting the land shape our days. At night, we would find rest in roadside hotels, our bodies weary but our spirits alive.

And so, over the next three years, Grace and I traveled across the country, immersing ourselves in the magical beauty of the land. We hiked through seven National Parks, explored endless deserts, and lost ourselves in countless national and state forests. Together, we covered over 1,000 miles, leaving our footprints across the whole expanse of the United States.

During this time, I unplugged from the world. I carried my phone only for emergencies, refusing to let distractions steal the moment. My only tether to others was a blog, a simple way to share my experience and reassure my loved ones that I hadn't been eaten by a mountain lion or joined a remote mountain spiritual cult. No texts. No social media.

My real connection was with Grace. She walked beside me, her paws tracing every mile, her body nestled against mine at night. But she was more than just a fellow traveller, she was my north star. She asked for nothing but presence, for me to be here, now, with her. And when the noise in my head threatened to drown me, when grief, doubt, and fear closed in, she reminded me: the way forward isn't through force or fear. It's through trust, surrender, and love.

Grace taught me to listen: to the land, to my own heart, to the rhythms of a world far older and wiser than my mind could comprehend. She showed me how to trust the unknown, how to let the journey unfold without needing to control it. She reminded me that no matter how lost I felt, I was never truly alone.

I had no idea how this journey would unfold. No map could have prepared me for how those trails would unravel me. Every step stripped away another layer, breaking me open at the deepest levels of my being. And through it all, Grace stayed by my side, loyal and unwavering, never questioning, never hesitating, offering only love.

THE TRAILMARKERS

ANSWER THE CALL

Take a deep breath.

Imagine yourself standing at the edge of a vast, ancient forest. The air is crisp with the scent of earth and cedar. Watery morning light filters through the towering trees, casting soft, dancing shadows across the mossy ground. Everything is still, yet pulsing with life. A hush of expectancy hovers in the air, as if even the leaves have gone quiet in anticipation.

Before you, a narrow path winds deeper into the trees. It feels familiar, though you've never walked it before. Something about it tugs at you, a silent beckoning. This is not just any path. It is your path. And it's waiting.

Can you hear it?

The call rising from deep within, like a steady pulsing drumbeat in the distance. At first, it's faint, but the longer you stand here, the louder it grows, reverberating through your cells. Insistent. Undeniable. You've heard it before—in dreams, in the silent spaces between your thoughts, in the longing that never quite faded.

And yet, you've turned away.
Buried it beneath to-do lists and obligations. Wrapped it in layers of fear and uncertainty.
But still, it waits.
Patient. Unwavering.

A soft wind quickens around you, carrying a message. It brushes your skin like a gentle nudge from the unseen:

"Step forward. Trust me. I will guide you."

Pause here. Breathe. Let the words settle in your body.
Ask yourself: What is my heart calling me toward... or away from? What steps am I ready to take to answer this call?

Trust whatever arises. There is no right or wrong, only information, waiting to be heard.

Now, feel the fear that comes with this pull.
It may crash over you like a wave, loud, overwhelming.

Or it may linger like a long shadow, whispering doubts that tighten your chest:

"What if I fail?"

"What if I choose the wrong path?"

You know this inner prompting is asking for more than you feel ready to give.
It demands that you face what you've buried, your deepest fears, your wounds, your long-forgotten dreams. It calls you into the wilderness of your own heart, mind, body, and soul—a place where you'll meet both the darkness you dread and the light you fear you'll never deserve.

Some days, it may feel like the air has been stolen from your lungs.
The fear urges you to stay where it's safe, where the unknown cannot reach.
But even as you hesitate, the call persists.

The path ahead will not be easy.
It will ask you to release what has outlived its purpose. To step beyond the barriers you've created. It will demand courage, vulnerability, and trust in the unseen.
But it will also bring restoration. Freedom.
And the unshakable knowing that you are exactly where you're meant to be.

Now, take a slow, deep breath.
Feel the energy of this moment land in your heart.
Know this: the calling is not separate from you.
It is you—your truth, your compass, your opportunity to begin again.

The path is before you.
All that's left is to begin.

THE CALL OF CHANGE

Not every call of the heart arrives as a personal memo from the universe. Some don't pull you toward something new, they urge you to walk away from what you've outgrown.

You're taught to wait for the big "yes"—the fire-in-the-belly kind of call, the vision that lights you up, the spark that makes your whole body buzz with excitement. And sometimes, it does come like that: a rising, a clarity, a deep yearning for more. A message from the depths rising up to say: *There is something else meant for you.*

But just as often, these nudges arrive in silence.
In discomfort.
In restlessness and anxiety.

Sometimes it shows up as a tightening in your chest or a clenching in your gut, the unmistakable feeling that the life you've built is no longer yours. The routines feel hollow. The roles you play feel like costumes. The conversations, the commitments, even the dreams you once held close, they all start to feel like they belong to someone else.

It's not a maybe.
It's a clear, embodied "NO."
Not this. Not anymore.

That no reverberated through every part of me, especially in the relationship I knew I needed to leave. The shape of my life no longer reflected the shape of my soul.

These are the calls we rarely talk about, the ones that don't ask you to pursue something, but to release it. To walk away from what's become too small, too painful, or too misaligned. And yet, they are just as essential as the calls that ignite the fire.

You may remember that first inner summons, undeniable and vivid. I know I do.

I was five years old when I knew I wanted to be an actress. Not in the fleeting way children dream of being astronauts or princesses, but with a conviction that felt bone-deep and unshakable. I could see it. I could feel it. My name in lights. The electric thrill of the stage. The magic of evoking emotion in others with a single line or glance. It wasn't just a dream, it was my destiny. And I chased it.

But what I didn't understand then is that the longings of your heart don't always follow a straight path. Mine led me through a maze of ambition, rejection, and hidden pain. The desire to express my natural gifts slowly gave way to the desperation to be chosen. I began trading pieces of myself for the reassurance of being seen, wanted and praised. I convinced myself these sacrifices were necessary. But each one pulled me further from my center.

Still, I can see now that it all had a purpose.
Even the detours held meaning.
Acting wasn't a mistake, it became a doorway to something new.
It led me to become a psychotherapist.

And when Grace came into my life, I answered another call.
This time, it wasn't about success.
It was about healing, stillness, freedom and truth.

Just as I had once followed the call to become someone, I now followed the call to *unbecome,* from a version of myself that felt confining, from an old identity that no longer felt like mine. I had to walk away from a career that drained me and from relationships that had stopped nourishing me. I stripped it all back, trusting that what remained would be real and true.

Every call I've ever answered, whether toward or away, has altered me.
They shattered illusions I once clung to.
They broke me open in places I didn't even know were locked.
They asked me to let go before I felt ready.
And through it all, they led me somewhere new.
Somewhere important.

The call of the heart is vital, but so is the struggle to answer it.

ARE YOU READY TO ANSWER?

When the heart calls, fear often answers first.
It's quick, insistent, and sounds something like this:
What if I'm not enough?
What if I lose everything?
Shouldn't I just be grateful?

Fear is persistent and clever. Sometimes it shouts. Sometimes it whispers. Sometimes it disguises itself as reason—masked as practicality, maturity, or caution. But the message is always the same: stay small, stay certain, stay safe.

You feel it in your body before you name it: a tight chest, a fluttering pulse, a knot in your belly. Your mind clouds. Doubt multiplies. The trail ahead blurs. But fear is not a stop sign, it's just part of the initiation. Its very presence means you're standing on the edge of a life larger than the one you know.

This is the turning point, where fear rises not to stop you, but to ask if you're ready.

Allow fear to walk beside you, just don't hand it the map. Acknowledge the tremor, hear the questions, then take one deliberate step. With each step taken in spite of fear, the ground beneath you shifts. You don't become fearless; you become bigger than your fear. And in doing so, you reclaim the territory inside yourself that it once occupied.

Fear will keep clamoring for your attention, but its intensity fades when your feet keep moving. Every breath you draw beyond that boundary becomes proof: you are doing something brave, living what is real, and choosing what truly matters.

But the harder question is this: *What happens if you don't answer the call?*

THE HAUNTING OF AN UNANSWERED CALL

Ignoring the call of your heart isn't a single act of defiance but a slow erosion, a series of small denials that chip away at the core of who you are.

Each time you turn away from that inner nudge, a part of you fades. The voice of your soul grows faint, buried beneath distractions, expectations, and everything you think you should be. But the hunger remains, a reminder that you've stepped off the path meant for you. At first, the world keeps you busy—tasks, comforts, and the constant chase for validation. You check the boxes, meet the deadlines, and perform the roles. You may even look successful from the outside. But when the noise settles, the misalignment lingers. You look in the mirror and see someone familiar, but distant. And the question begins to haunt you: *Is this who I'm meant to be?*

Misalignment feels like walking against a relentless wind. You show up where you're expected, do what needs to be done, and smile at the right moments. On the surface, it looks like you've got everything under control. But inside, a quiet exhaustion grows heavier by the day.

Your relationships begin to suffer because you're no longer fully present. Your work feels unfulfilling, disconnected from any sense of purpose. And the weight of everything unspoken, everything you've swallowed just to hold things together, becomes unbearable.

No amount of success, praise, or approval can fill the void that comes from betraying yourself. The only way back to alignment is through—through the discomfort of admitting where you've strayed, the courage to step into the unfamiliar, and the commitment to reclaim the life that has always been yours.

Coming into alignment is a kind of homecoming. It often begins quietly, when your outer life starts to reflect what you've always known in your heart. It's choosing to listen to the inner whispers, even when they ask you to release what feels safe. It's saying yes to what's real for you, even when fear urges you to be cautious, to settle, or to hold yourself back.

Answering the call demands more than courage, it demands surrender. Letting go of control. Trusting the mystery of what you can't yet see. These inner nudges don't always make sense. It's not tidy or convenient. It's raw, visceral, and at times terrifying. But it is also your clearest guide, leading you toward what is most important.

To ignore it is to turn your back on yourself.
To follow it is to reclaim your life, piece by piece.
To step out of the shadows of compromise and into the light of what's real.

To answer the call of your heart is to come alive. The path won't be easy, but it will feel right. A current of clarity moves through you as your life begins to align with your truest self. It is the joy of waking to a life that mirrors your soul, a deep knowing that you've stopped shrinking, apologizing, and hiding.

These calls are relentless because they are the essence of who you are. They beckon you to step fully into yourself—to love deeply and live boldly. They remind you that you are not here to fit a mold, but to create, inspire, and lead. And when you follow this inner urging, it doesn't just change you, it changes everything around you.

RIPPLES

Every call arrives with a crossroads—a moment to choose, to act, to decide what stays and what must go. And while it's tempting to believe those decisions are yours alone, no call happens in isolation. Each choice you make ripples outward, touching the lives entwined with your own. The people you love—partners, friends, family, community—are each navigating their own inner summons, their own thresholds of pain and possibility. Sometimes their path is to stay when you know you must go. Sometimes their path is to leave while you're still holding on.

You've likely felt every edge of that tension. Perhaps you were blindsided when someone you trusted chose to walk away. Or you lingered too long, hoping they'd hear the same pull you did, only to discover you had to journey on alone. You may have watched people you love remain in places that were breaking them, feeling powerless to pull them out. And perhaps you've been the one holding someone back, staying silent when you should've urged them forward. Afraid to lose them. Afraid to change.

I know this struggle intimately; I've lived in all of these spaces, where the weight of others' choices collided with my own inner knowing and deepest desires.

Our lives are always intersecting—shaping, shifting, influencing each other's paths. A loved one's fear can hold you still. A friend's courage can become your mirror. A partner's silence, a parent's pain, a stranger's unexpected kindness, any of it can become your turning point.

You can't control how others respond to their calling. But you can choose how you respond to yours. You can refuse to let someone else's fear become your own. You can honor your inner guidance, even when it asks you to walk away. And you can trust that you are never truly alone, that unexpected helpers and unseen guides will meet you along the way.

Answering your call, while witnessing theirs, is never easy. It breaks you open. It asks you to release your grip before you know what will catch you. But staying stuck breaks you too, only more quietly and more slowly. As the life you thought you wanted unravels, a deeper ache rises—the relentless longing beneath a life unlived.

And when you finally face that fear, you find a strength that's reliable and resolute. A knowing that while you may lose what is familiar, you are reclaiming something far more essential. You don't leap because you can see the other side. You leap because the pain of staying has grown heavier than the risk of leaving. Because you are ready to grow wings. And when you do, your courage becomes a ripple. An unspoken permission. A light for others still standing at the edge.

Dear Fellow Journeyer,

There is a voice within you, quiet yet persistent, soft yet unwavering. It doesn't demand, but gently invites. It calls you toward something deeper, truer, and uniquely yours. This is the call of your heart, the essence of your soul urging you to remember who you are and why you're here.

Answering this call is an act of bravery.

It asks you to face your fears, shed the layers that no longer reflect who you are, and trust the unknown. It means letting go of the stories others have written for you, so you can finally author your own life, one led by inner authority. This path isn't easy, but it's the only one that leads to the fullness of life, to the wisdom that has always lived within you.

Your heart's urging is yours alone. It's a map written in the language of your desires, dreams, and deepest longings. No one else can walk this path for you. Only you can uncover the gifts it holds. But here's what matters most: You're not searching for something outside yourself, you're remembering what has always been within. And when you find the courage to answer, you step into alignment with the boundless, infinite potential of your own spirit.

Let me remind you: Your heart is not wrong.

It knows the way, even when your mind doesn't yet understand the destination. When you stay in alignment, the right doors open, the right people appear, and the right opportunities unfold.

Don't trade honesty for safety, or diminish yourself to be loved. You don't need to be less to belong. The world doesn't need the version of you defined by fear. It needs the one who dares to love, dream, and shine boldly.

So, dear one, listen to the call.

Honor the wild ache in your chest and the quiet knowing in your core. It is your compass, your guide, your sanctuary.

You are capable.
You are worthy.

You are enough.

Take a brave step with all the courage your heart can muster, and watch as the world rearranges itself to meet you.

As you move forward, ask yourself:
What is the call of my heart today?

It won't lead you away from yourself, but straight home.
Trust your knowing.
Trust the process.
And most of all, trust yourself.

TRAIL WISDOM

ANSWER THE CALL

The call of your heart won't always be loud, but it will always be true.
You don't need certainty, just courage.
Fear may walk beside you, but it doesn't get to lead.
Let go of what no longer fits.

Release the weight of who you thought you had to be.
Take one brave step, no matter how small.
The path will meet you there, rising to greet you with every step you dare to take.

THE TRAILHEAD

Take a deep breath.

Imagine you're standing at the edge of a new trail, where the path behind you softens into memory and the unknown stretches wide before you. The ground beneath your feet is solid yet untouched, a doorway between what has been and what is yet to come. The air is laced with the scent of mossy earth and wild blooms—violet and buttercup bowing gently to the breeze. Sunlight filters through drifting clouds, casting a radiant glow across the landscape ahead.

This is your trailhead.
A place where one journey ends and another begins.
A gateway to possibility.

Behind you lies the well-worn path of familiarity—past decisions, known rhythms, and the predictable comforts of what has been. But ahead, the trail diverges: some paths meander through open meadows; others wind into hills or vanish into shadowed forests. A few are clear and inviting. Others are faint, nearly hidden, their destinations cloaked in mystery.

You linger here, heart thudding with quiet anticipation.
You know a choice must be made.

You could remain rooted in the safety of the familiar.
Or you could step forward, into the promise of what's yet to be.

The wind stirs the tall grasses beside you, summoning you to trust, to move, to follow the call that has been quietly rising from within.

You close your eyes. You listen—to the rustling leaves, to the distant murmur of the wild, to the steady beat within your chest.
And beneath the hesitation and fear, something enduring remains.
A knowing. A truth too important to deny.

Here you stand, at your trailhead.
Not just a beginning, but a return.
A remembrance.
An awakening.
And with your next step, the path becomes yours.

THE PATH AWAITS

Life is marked by trailheads, those in-between moments when one part of your journey ends and another begins. Whatever the reason or pull for change, the trailhead appears in the moment you make a hard decision, or in the pause before you take the first step in a new direction.

At the start of the trail, you stand at the threshold of a path you cannot yet fully comprehend. Faced with the vastness of the unknown, your heart hesitates. Your mind questions. And yet, you take the next step, because once you choose to seek aliveness, there is no going back.

Some paths stretch wide and luminous, brimming with new horizons; others are steep and tangled, demanding courage before offering reward. Yet every trail you walk, no matter how winding, shapes you. And as you attune to the rhythm of your footfalls, to the quiet between labored breaths, something becomes clear: You were never meant to stay still. You are built to move, seek, and grow.

Trailheads are the universe's way of pulling you forward, inviting you to evolve, to step toward what you do not yet know, but sense has always been waiting.

Sometimes, when you ignore the quiet nudges, the choice is made for you.
The job loss. The sudden ending. The unexpected upheaval.
It can feel like collapse, like the ground has been ripped out from beneath you.
It shakes the structures you've built, the things you've clung to, the illusions you've wrapped around your life for safety. But more often than not, it's also a clearing, a Divine rupture that creates space for what's next. A forced surrender to what your soul already knows is needed.

The question is this: *Will you honor the nudge while it's still a whisper, or wait until it hits you over the head?*

When you finally make the monumental choice, the world should shift, shouldn't it? You expect clarity, or at least a sign that you've done the right thing.
But more often, there is only silence.
No confirmation. No blessing. Just stillness.
It is here, in the space between what was and what will be, that fear slips in.
Your mind, so loyal to the known, begins to protest.

Turn back, it murmurs. *You were safer before.*

This is the wilderness between two lives, the place after the old has been left behind, but before the new has fully arrived. The void where fear breeds doubt, where the shadows of your past rise up to test your resolve. The ground beneath you feels unsteady, trembling under the seismic choice to disrupt the life you knew.

So you bargain and rationalize. You tell yourself you were impulsive, that you should wait for a better time, for more certainty, for a cosmic permission slip that will never come. You convince yourself the call was a passing whim, or worse, that you imagined it altogether.

But stepping forward requires risk, and risk threatens your sense of safety. You are wired for comfort, easily drawn to the familiar even when it stifles you, because at least it's predictable. To risk is to enter the unimagined. To open yourself to loss, rejection, and the terrifying truth that things may not unfold as you hoped. Risk is standing on the bridge between worlds, made not of stone, but of air and faith. The kind of faith that trusts that the support will appear the moment you step forward.

Every choice brings change, and with it, an awakening.
A reckoning with how you arrived here.

You're now on a path of consciousness, one that asks you to release what you've outgrown. To transmute what once felt like safety but now rings hollow. To turn toward long-repressed feelings and unearth forgotten dreams.

So, yes, you hesitate at the trailhead, unsure if you're ready.
But beneath the fear, something truer breathes to life.
A soft, persistent voice rises from within.
This is the way, it says. *Keep going.*
And so you do, cautiously or boldly.
You take a deep breath.
And step onto the path.

STANDING AT THE EDGE

Throughout my journey, there were many trailheads pulling me forward, each one a fresh beginning, revealing another layer of who I thought I was. But the first one held the most significance. It asked me to draw from the deepest reservoir of willingness and courage I had ever known, to leap into unfamiliar territory without a map or itinerary, and trust my heart to guide me, no matter where the trail might lead.

My three-year wilderness walk began at a single spot on the Appalachian Trail near Pen Mar Park in Maryland. Part of me was exhilarated by all this journey might offer; part of me was terrified. I was about to trek into the void with nothing but a backpack, a hopeful heart, and what I thought was adequate preparation. (Spoiler alert: no amount of YouTube videos, wilderness classes, or checklists can prepare you for soul excavation.)

A simple wooden post, weathered by time and the elements, marked the beginning of the trail, twisting into the shadows of the forest ahead. On the post, a single blue marker pointing straight forward. No instructions. No pressure. Just a quiet, unwavering nudge, perhaps from the universe itself, to go this way instead of going back.

The air around me shifted, swirling like it was charged with invisible electricity. Shivers danced along my spine. I inhaled the scent of sweet grass and pine bark, rich and grounding, as if the land itself held the promise of my transformation. Behind me lay a well-worn road, familiar faces and places I knew like the back of my hand. Ahead of me, certainty dissolved into mystery.

My chest tightened. Fear settled into my body, cold and heavy, as my mind raced with reasons to turn back.
What if I can't handle it?
What if I unravel completely... and there's nothing left to find?
What if what's ahead is even harder than what I've left behind?
What if I die?

The gravity of those thoughts threatened to paralyze me. But beneath the fear, something deeper stirred, small, but unyielding: hope. Caught between fear and hope, I turned to what I could see, trusting the earth to offer clarity where my mind couldn't.

I stood frozen at the trailhead, my mind scrambling for reasons to stay behind. Then I looked down—*really* looked. At the hard-packed dirt. The roots crossing the path. The pine needles scattered like offerings underfoot. I couldn't see far, just a bend up ahead, where the trees thickened and the light began to fade.

Something about that bend called to me. Maybe I'd find a version of myself that felt free and unburdened. Alive in a way I hadn't known before. A life that felt deeply aligned and meaningful. A morning where I could wake up without that constant, low-grade anxiety that had followed me for years.

I thought of everything I was leaving behind:
Friendships that had once felt grounding but had begun to drift, held together more by shared history than shared values. Work that had once felt purposeful, but had started to slowly drain the life from me. The routines I once relied on, overbooked calendars, rigid habits, nonstop motion that gave me a sense of control, now just felt empty. They kept me moving, but not connected.

Standing there, I realized I wasn't really afraid of the unknown path ahead. I was afraid of how much I wanted to take it. Afraid to admit that the life I'd carefully constructed was no longer the life I wanted to live.

Even as my body hesitated, something deeper had already begun moving forward. It had answered the call long before my feet arrived here, before the air had shifted, before the forest had breathed my name. My heart had been leading me all along, asking to serve as the compass that could guide me through the wilderness I had yet to face.

As I reconnected with that gut knowing, I felt hope rise again. I wondered: *What might be waiting on the other side if I had the courage to trust the pull of my heart?*

Beside me, Grace stood alert but at ease, ears twitching at the rustling leaves. She didn't resist, she rarely did. She simply existed in the now, bound by no past, unafraid of the uncharted land stretching before us. She was everything I longed to be, wild and untethered, trusting the moment, moving forward with instinct and unwavering faith. She embodied the freedom meant for me, if only I could be as fearless as she was.

Grace nudged my hand, sensing the storm within me. Then she took a step, no hesitation or doubt. I closed my eyes, exhaled slowly, and followed. The trail softened beneath my boots—quiet, forgiving, as if it had been waiting for me all along.

THE WEIGHT WE CARRY

We all carry a backpack through life. Some things are slung casually over one shoulder. Others, strapped on tight, as if a looser fit might mean losing control. No one else can see it, but you feel its weight with every step you take. Some of what you carry is beautiful—reminders of love, moments of celebration, the lessons that made you wiser. But depending on your wounds, traumas, and betrayals, that backpack can also be incredibly heavy.

At first, you don't question what's inside. You pack it as you grow, first with childhood memories, then with life's experiences and heartbreaks. Over time, it becomes heavier, filled not just with what you've lived through, but also with what you've held on to. Some of it you placed there yourself. And some was handed to you by others: words that cut deep, rejections that left scars, beliefs you never questioned, lessons you seemingly never asked to learn.

For some, the backpack is well-worn, edges frayed from years of carrying burdens that were never meant to be permanent. For others, it appears untouched, pristine on the outside—but inside, everything is crumpled, torn, and stuffed away haphazardly, as if hiding the damage might make it disappear.

The heaviest things are often the ones you don't talk about.
The father who left.
The betrayal you never saw coming.
The love that was given and then taken away.
The moment you stopped believing you were enough.

These wounds sit at the bottom of your pack, tucked into secret compartments, weighing you down even when you pretend they aren't there. Some things you've carried for so long, you can no longer tell where the weight ends and you begin. You come to believe this burden is simply a part of you, an integral aspect of who you are, rather than a reflection of how you coped with what life handed you.

And still, you're terrified to set it down.
Because who would you be without it?

If you let go of the pain, the stories, the survival mechanisms—would you still recognize yourself? You tell yourself the past made you stronger. That you carry this load because you must. Because it's what you know.

But deep down, you sense the truth:
It's not strength that keeps you holding on.
It's fear.

So you keep walking, adjusting the straps, shifting the weight from one shoulder to the other, trying to move forward despite the exhaustion. But you feel it in your body, the fatigue, the hesitation, the way joy seems just out of reach. You wonder why you feel stuck, why your dreams feel impossible, why fulfillment remains elusive.

Your backpack might hold suppressed dreams, packed away neatly with the promise of *someday.*
A novel never written.
A passion never pursued.
A version of yourself you denied because someone once told you it was impractical.

Maybe your pack holds grief, unprocessed and heavy, filling the space where peace was meant to live. Or perhaps it carries abuse, zipped up tightly, making trust feel impossible. Some backpacks are old and tattered, their history visible in every faded stitch. Others appear shiny and new, carefully curated so no one suspects the frayed edges within. Some have hidden pockets where pain hides behind the seams, buttoned up and forgotten, until it isn't. Some are adorned with patches and stickers, outward markers of the things you've survived or the identities you've clung to.

No two backpacks are the same. But no matter how different they look, they all carry the same fundamental truth: You cannot walk freely toward your future while dragging the past behind you.

At some point, you must stop and ask yourself:
Do I really want to keep carrying this?
Is there anything I can unpack along the way?

Because the path ahead is long and the lighter you travel, the farther you can go. And perhaps, just perhaps, your real strength isn't found in carrying more, but in discerning what's no longer needed.

MY VOW

For a long time, I didn't question what was in my backpack. I carried it because it was mine, because I always had. I assumed that was just how life worked. Some burdens are assigned to us, unavoidable and inescapable.

I had grown used to its weight, convinced it would always be there, as much a part of me as my own skin. But as I stepped beyond the trailhead, the heaviness became impossible to ignore, the ache in my shoulders, the pressure on my spine, the struggle to breathe beneath its load.

It wasn't until I finally stopped—*really stopped*—to take stock of what I was carrying that I began to see it clearly for the first time.

And here's what I found.

The devastation of childhood cruelty: the boy next door who taunted and threatened me. His intense, unpredictable anger that often left me frozen. I remember counting the seconds as I ran home from school, desperate to make it inside before he saw me.

But it wasn't just him. His father was worse. A man full of resentment toward my parents, and a bitter hatred for our animals. His rage didn't erupt all at once, it built slowly, little by little. Seething beneath the surface. Until one day, it turned into action.

He began taking the lives of some of our animals, first a horse, then dogs, one by one. Not in a single violent outburst, but over time. Always denying it, of course. But I knew. Each loss cut deeper than the last. Each one chipped away at my innocence.

Then there was the silence that followed the disappearance of my horse, sold without warning. The one soul who made me feel truly loved was gone before I even had the chance to say goodbye.

Fear and loss didn't just stop at the edge of the yard. They lived inside our home, too. My father's rage was a storm I never knew how to prepare for.
His voice, like thunder.
His presence, a cloud always threatening to rain down discontent and

disappointment.

I learned to shrink, to step lightly, to brace for the explosion.

I took on the impossible task of protecting my older sister from his fury, believing it was my job to keep her safe. That same sister's jealousy hit hard, her anger, cruel at times. Words like "Daddy's favorite" and "princess" flung like arrows. They got to me more than I wanted to admit. And under all of it lived a guilt I couldn't shake: the guilt of being the one he spared. The one who somehow escaped the full force of his wrath.

My mother's love came in fragments, sometimes warm, sometimes absent. Predictable in its unpredictability. I learned not to ask for too much. I taught myself that self reliance was safer than disappointment.

It took me years to understand: she was carrying her *own* backpack. The emotional abuse by my father. The loneliness that sometimes swallowed her whole. And the grief of needs left unmet, not out of neglect, but because those around her didn't have the capacity to give what she needed.

And yet, tucked beside the heartbreak, we found the beginning of our healing.
The way we slowly found our way back to each other.
The laughter that cracked open old pain.
The honesty that aired out long-held wounds.
The small but unforgettable moments, meditating side by side, holding hands on quiet mornings, that reminded me love, even when flawed, can still find its way home.

It wasn't just other people I carried. It was what their inconsistent love and absence taught me to believe about myself.
That I had to earn love.
That my needs were too much.
That I had to hold it all together to be accepted.

The exhaustion of trying to be everything for everyone.
Of twisting myself to fit into spaces never meant for me.
The silent plea for approval hidden in every smile.
The pieces of myself I abandoned just to be liked.

And alongside all of that was the weight of dreams that never came true, moments when I stood at the edge of something big but couldn't find the courage to leap.

There was also my body.
The one that turned on me.
The one that became a battlefield.
The autoimmune disease was the evidence, undeniable proof of what happens when you carry too much for too long. My body had been warning me for years. But I didn't listen. So eventually, it had no choice. It began to scream.

Tucked deeply in my pack was something just as heavy, the wreckage of my romantic relationships. Years of trying to make broken things whole.
Mistaking pain for passion.
Choosing chaos over calm, because calm felt unfamiliar.

I didn't know how to grieve, so I didn't. I packed the sadness away, shoved it down deep where I wouldn't have to feel it.
The anger buried itself.
The resentment curled into hidden corners.

But that wasn't the whole story.
My pack held more than suffering.
It also held the quiet, unwavering love of friends who stayed.
The unconditional presence of animals nestled beside me on my loneliest nights.
The gift of my grandparents, their love stitched into meals, memories, and the smell of corned beef and cabbage simmering on the stove.

It held the joy of curiosity.
The freedom of exploration.
The sparks of inspiration that showed me there's another way to guide others through their healing, one that would honor my soul.

So, as the path stretched ahead, I made a vow:
To turn and face it all—the grief, the fear, the buried hurt.
To let go of what no longer belongs.

To take off the weight I've carried for too long:
The pattern of attempting to love those who could never love me back.
The impact of slammed doors.
The pain of never being a priority.
The belief that I am not enough.
To lighten the load. And finally allow myself the grace to exhale.

Dear Fellow Journeyer,

I see you there, heart full of questions, mind swirling with fear.
This moment—this threshold—is no small thing.
It marks the shift from what has been to what could be.
It's the place where you decide, even with trembling hands and a pounding heart, to begin again.

I know what it feels like to shoulder so much.
For so long, I adjusted and readjusted, trying to hold it all.
Every lesson, every heartbreak, and every shadow felt like mine to bear.
I convinced myself I had to keep going, to prove I could carry it all.
Each piece became a badge of survival, proof of where I'd been.
Letting any of it go felt impossible.

But deep down, I knew:
If I didn't begin to release the load, it would eventually pull me under. So, just beyond that trailhead, with the first few steps behind me and the unknown stretching wide ahead, I started to loosen my grip.

Some of what you hold was never yours, passed down by others through silence, expectation, or pain. Some of it you picked up just trying to make it through.
But not everything you've packed is meant to go with you.
Some things were only meant for a season.
Others were never meant to be yours at all.

Still, you cling, afraid that letting go might mean losing a part of yourself.
Because when something has been with you for so long, even pain can feel familiar.

But here's what I know:
You are not defined by what you carry.

You're allowed to pause.
To unpack.
To hold each piece in your hands and ask:
Do I still need this?
Is it keeping me safe or keeping me hidden?
Is it even mine to hold?

You're allowed to walk lighter.
To set things down.

The gateways in our lives are life giving.
They arrive when the old path is no longer yours to walk—
when life begins to feel too narrow for the person you're becoming.

They aren't just beginnings; they're portals back to yourself.
To move toward freedom, alignment, and the deeper parts of you waiting to be
remembered.

And yes, it takes courage to stand here.
Uncertainty can feel overwhelming.
Doubt will try to lure you back.

Yet beneath the fear is a quieter voice—loving and true—reminding you:
There is more for you here.

Just by arriving at this moment, you've already proven your strength.
You don't need to have it all figured out.
You have this map.
You just need the willingness to begin.
To trust that what lies ahead holds more than what you're leaving behind.

There will be steep descents, tangled climbs, and days that test your will.
But there will also be clarity.
Resilience.
And flashes of light that remind you why you chose this path.

And if you're scared, that's okay.
If you don't know where it leads, that's okay too.

What matters is that you make that first move.
Because only by walking can you discover not just the road ahead, but the strength
you've earned, and the wisdom etched into your being by everything you've survived.
You are not alone.
I've stood here too, unsure, afraid, and still willing.
There are many of us on this path, each carving a way forward, connected by the
courage it takes to say yes to the journey.

So take a deep breath.
Look ahead.
And move.

The way forward may be uncertain, but it is also full of wonder, growth, and the kind of aliveness that only comes when you believe in yourself.

Trust the unfolding.
The path will rise to meet you.

TRAIL WISDOM

WALK YOUR OWN PATH

There will come a moment when the well-worn roads no longer call to you—
when the life you've built begins to feel too small for the truth rising inside.

This moment is not an ending, it's an invitation.
You were made to listen deeply, to choose boldly, and to walk the way only your
soul can see.

Trust the quiet pull.
Honor what awakens within you.
The wilderness may feel vast,
but it's where your true path begins.

And as you walk, you may discover that your backpack is heavier than it
needs to be.
Take time to pause.
Shift the weight.
Let go of what you no longer need.

The lighter you travel,
the more freely you can move through the world.

MEET YOUR GUIDES

Take a deep breath.

Imagine yourself beneath a towering canopy of ancient trees, their branches arcing high above like the vaulted ceiling of a sacred temple. The air is brisk and alive, carrying the scent of pine needles and the faint sweetness of honeysuckle hidden in the undergrowth. Shafts of sunlight pierce through the foliage, painting the forest floor in shifting patterns of light and shadow. As the warmth kisses your skin, a subtle sense of curiosity arises within you.

A narrow path winds ahead, barely visible between moss-covered roots and the ferns that sway gently, as if whispering encouragement. You take a step. Then another. The soft earth cradles your feet, grounding you more deeply with each movement.

Around you, the forest buzzes with life, the rhythmic rustling of leaves moved by an unseen breeze, the distant trill of a bird calling from the treetops, the soft gurgling of a stream hidden somewhere beyond the trees. The deeper you go, the more the world behind you fades, replaced by a profound stillness. And in that quiet, you begin to have the strangest sense that something, or even perhaps someone, is waiting.

The path opens into a clearing, where a pristine lake stretches wide before you, its surface so still it mirrors the sky above. A thin mist hangs over the water, moving slowly in the stillness of morning. You step closer, drawn to the edge, and peer into the depths.

At first, you see only your reflection, the soft curve of your face, those eyes that have witnessed so much.

But then, the water shifts.
Shapes emerge.
Forms appear beside you.

Your guides have arrived.

They stand with you, not as strangers, but as beings who have always been near. Some may be ancestors, their ancient eyes filled with stories, their presence wrapped in the scent of time and memory. Others might be spirit animals, their gaze intense, protective, and knowing. Still others could be teachers, radiating warmth, their hands open with guidance. Or maybe, they are something formless—a presence, a living energy that lets you know you're not alone.

They have been walking with you all along.

Feel them now. Their energy surrounds you, weaving through the trees, the air, the earth beneath your feet. It fills the spaces inside you that have longed for connection.

Take a breath. Listen.

What do they wish for you to know? What messages do they carry?

Breathe in the energy of their wise, loving presence. Let it anchor in your body, and settle deep into your spirit.

UNEXPECTED TEACHERS ALONG THE PATH

The journey through life is not meant to be walked in isolation. At every bend in the road, at every fork in the path, guides appear. Sometimes they arrive as seasoned mentors. Other times, as messages from your ancestors, or loved ones who have passed on. And often, as forgotten aspects of yourself, quietly waiting to be remembered. Each one carries wisdom, if you are open enough to feel it, hear it, and receive it.

The oldest and most enduring guides are your ancestral ones, living within your bloodlines. They breathe through your stories, move through your instincts, and speak through your dreams. Whether you know their names or not, their love and their pain have been passed down through generations, carried in your DNA, your traditions, and even your struggles. You may be called to break cycles, to heal what has long remained unspoken, and to honor the paths of those who came before. And in doing so, you do not heal alone, you heal your lineage, both past and future.

Some guides arrive in flesh and form, mentors who appear just when you're ready to receive them. They may be teachers, elders, friends, or even strangers who illuminate what you cannot yet see. They help you navigate uncertainty, share hard-earned wisdom, and remind you of your own strength. A true mentor doesn't offer answers, they ask the questions that awaken your truth. Their presence reminds you that you are not the first to step into the great unknown. Others have braved the wilderness and returned with teachings to share.

But not all guidance comes from outside you.
Some of the most insightful teachers live within.

The child who still remembers how to dream, create, and feel deeply without apology. The shadow, holding the truths you've buried, the lessons you've been too afraid to face. The future self, standing just ahead, calling you forward with loving encouragement. And the inner guide, whose voice has been with you all along, waiting patiently beneath the noise of the world, longing to lead you home.

Not all guidance feels like love at first. Some of it arrives disguised as pain, showing up through heartbreak, loss, conflict, or fear. These shadow teachers don't offer comfort, they offer initiation.

They break you open.
They sharpen your truth.
They reveal what still needs your attention.
Pain brings a clarity you rarely find elsewhere.
It strips away illusion and leads you back to the parts of yourself you've left behind.
Even your adversaries can become mirrors, reflecting what you're finally ready to release, reclaim, or rise above.

And just as some guides challenge you through fire, others arrive quietly, subtle and unseen, but deeply felt. Spirit guides move through your life like signals on the wind, ancient allies who walk beside you, teaching and protecting you.

They don't always appear in ways you expect. They can come as animals crossing your path at just the right moment. Other times, they speak through the pages of a book, a familiar song, a moment of synchronicity, or a deep inner resonance. And sometimes, they are simply unseen forces, a presence felt in stillness, a knowing that you are being watched over, a gentle push in the direction you're meant to go.

Guides and support are everywhere. They remind you that your path is not solely your own to navigate. It is informed by those who walked the path ahead of you, those who walk beside you now, and those who will follow long after you are gone. At times, they are a firm hand reaching through the dark. In other moments, they are the voice that calls you to rise, to see beyond your fear, to step forward when every part of you wants to retreat. There are also times when they ask nothing of you at all. They simply sit beside you—no words, no answers, just support. Holding space when you don't yet know how to hold it for yourself.

Still, you may see accepting help as a weakness.
A flaw.
A burden you're meant to carry alone.
But seeking guidance is not weakness, it's discernment.
It takes strength to admit you can't deal with it all yourself.
It takes even more to let yourself be seen, uplifted, and held.

When you shut out support, whether from others or from your own inner guidance, you close yourself off from the very growth and connection you most need. But when you open to it, you're woven into something far larger than yourself. You remember that you are not separate. You are part of a living story, one that began long before you and will continue long after.

I learned this not just through study or belief, but through my own journey. My teachers and guides carried me when I had no strength to walk. When I could stand again, they walked beside me. And when the time came, they stepped back and let me go, trusting that I would find my own way.

I met them all on my journey—my inner child, my shadow, my future self, my ancestors, my mentors, and my spirit guides. When I got still enough, they were there, waiting to meet me on the path. And sometimes, those meetings came in the most unexpected ways, offering clues, insights, and quiet affirmations when I needed them most.

Some of the most beautiful moments on the trail happened because I had no set destination. Without an itinerary, I moved in a different kind of rhythm, one not only dictated by miles or markers, but by instinct, intuition, and unexpected encounters. I'd meet someone along the path, and they'd speak of an experience, place, or memory. A hidden lake. A quiet overlook with amazing sunsets. A grove where the light filtered through just right in the late afternoon.

As we hiked, we also shared stories, not just of the trail, but of the internal journeys that had brought us there. It became clear that in some way, we were all navigating our own wilderness within. Some were fresh out of relationships, trying to heal their heartbreak. Others were leaving behind careers, unsure what came next. Some felt completely lost, searching for meaning or direction. And a few were finally facing deep traumas they had long buried, now rising to the surface like roots breaking through soil.

These moments felt like breadcrumbs, gently guiding me in directions I hadn't considered. And more often than not, following them led me somewhere meaningful—physically, emotionally, spiritually. Not because it was on a map, but because I allowed myself to be led. There was something magical about living that way, open, unattached, willing to trust the unfolding. It wasn't aimless. It was intentional in its surrender. And in that space, life met me with wonder, connection, and the quiet assurance that I was exactly where I was meant to be.

Those experiences deepened my connection to all of my guides.
It helped me understand, more deeply than ever, that I have never been alone.
I only needed to slow down and be still enough to listen.

What I discovered wasn't just for me.
And I know now, it's not just my story. It's also yours.

You are traveling your own path, shaped by your own stories, yet moving toward the same sacred return. Your trail may twist in unexpected ways, and your challenges may not always look like mine, but you are bound by something greater than you can see. Even across the seeming distance of space and time, I feel the thread that holds us.

And so I want you to know:
I am here.
With you.
For you.

In the end, we are always guiding each other, sometimes knowingly, sometimes without even realizing it. It is only pride and fear that keep us closed, that make us forget how deeply connected we truly are, not just through shared stories or lived experience, but through something more fundamental. A woven strand of indivisible interconnection that runs beneath the surface of our separateness. And beneath it all, we are a part of the same great unfolding, the same evolution of consciousness that births worlds.

I am grateful for those who have shown me the way, for how their presence became a lantern on my path. Their love, their insight, even their challenges shaped me. They reminded me of who I am, and who I am becoming.

The wilderness is immense.
But you do not wander it alone.
There are footprints ahead of you, voices behind you, and light within you.
You are held.
You are guided.
And one day, you too will become the light for those who follow.

THE CHILD WITHIN

As you walk the path through the wilderness, it will eventually bring you to a quieter place, the tender terrain of memory, emotion, and ingenuity. There, waiting in the shadows, is the child who remembers who you were before the world asked you to forget.

Your inner child is not just a memory of who you once were, it is a living presence within you. A guide carrying truths you may have forgotten. It holds the essence of your joy, your wonder, and your unfiltered expression. It remembers the dreams that once came effortlessly, the emotions you embraced without shame, and the creative imagination that found magic in the simplest things.

But this younger self also carries the wounds, the moments you were unseen, unheard, or made to feel inadequate. It holds the times you had to be strong when all you wanted was to be held, the ways you learned to suppress your needs just so no one got upset. It carries the pain of being told you were too much or not enough. And though you have grown, those experiences still live in the places where you doubt yourself, silence your voice, or question whether you're worthy of love.

Beyond these surface wounds are deeper imprints, the betrayals that fractured your trust, the losses that hollowed you out, and the despair that informed your survival. This tender part of you has carried it all quietly for years, waiting for the moment you would finally turn toward it with the understanding and care it always needed.

But it does not simply wait, it beckons. It longs to be acknowledged, to be received, and finally have what it was once denied. Yet too often, instead of tending to it, you replay the abandonment within yourself, neglecting or judging the parts of you that yearn for nurturing and tenderness. And when this child within you feels invisible, it acts out, informing your choices, influencing your relationships—not from a place of wholeness but from its unmet pain. It may demand, push, or grasp for what was once withheld, hoping others will fill a void only you can truly tend to.

Still, within these wounds lies something deeper. This younger self holds the key to where you are being called to heal. It knows exactly what most needs your attention. Every pang of doubt, every place where you feel small, every fear that rises within you—that is your inner child pointing to the places still longing for compassion.

This part of you is not here to keep you bound to the past, but to lead you home to yourself. It calls you to reclaim what was left behind, the spontaneous laughter, the uninhibited creativity, the ability to feel fully and love without hesitation. It reminds you that play is not frivolous but a return to joy. That feeling deeply is not a limitation, but aliveness. That the parts of you the world once rejected are the very pieces that make you whole.

This child within is not lost. It has never left. It has always been here, waiting for you to find your way back. And when you finally take its hand, you will remember the truth: You were never broken. You were only awakening.

To truly understand this inner child, you must first remember what shaped them. What they feared. What they carried. And what they learned to hide in order to survive.

WHEN THE LIGHTS WENT OUT

The dark had a pulse. I could feel it thudding beneath my bed, sliding behind the closet door, pressing against the windows where the tree branches scraped like clawed hands trying to get in. It wasn't just empty space, it was alive. Watching. Breathing. And it saw me.

I dreaded nightfall. I begged my parents to leave the light on, but the answer never changed, a tired sigh, a flick of the switch, their footsteps retreating down the hall. Light drained from my walls, swallowed by the corners where the monsters waited.

I pulled my stuffed animals close, tucking them under my chin, careful to keep them from the edge of the bed. I was their only protection. If even one paw or floppy ear slipped over the side, the beast underneath would take them. I was sure of it. The space beneath the bed was a mouth, wide and waiting, ready to devour anything foolish enough to come too close.

Across the room, the dolls and clowns perched on the small rocking chair offered no comfort. Their glass eyes caught the moonlight, vacant and fixed. Their painted lips poised to speak if I stared too long.

If one of my animals fell, a bear tumbling off the edge, a rabbit sliding to the floor, I would lunge, heart hammering, and snatch them back before the monster could grab them. My arms were their shield. My hands, their salvation. I held them close and whispered against their worn fur, *You're safe. As long as you stay with me, you're safe.*

And that's when the sounds began. The wind threaded through the window frame, whistling so faintly it almost formed a voice. The clock on my nightstand ticked, too loud, too slow. A thud from the attic. Then the footsteps. Not those of my parents whose solid, familiar steps I could recognize anywhere. These were different. Hollow. Weightless. Like someone moving just out of view. They echoed down the hall in the dead of night, slow and deliberate, like something waiting for me in the dark.

I froze, breath held, every muscle locked.
Had I really heard it? Or was the dark playing tricks on me?

Silence followed. The kind that doesn't just fill the room, but listens back. I wanted to call out, but my throat tightened. If I made a sound, it might find me. The quiet after my parents' voices faded cut like a knife, sharp and merciless.

Worse than shadows. Worse than scratching branches.

Because in that silence, I was alone.

The nightmares always found me. They dragged me under, deeper than sleep, to a place where things with too many arms reached for me, and where voices muttered in a language I didn't understand. I woke up gasping, drenched in sweat, terror clenching my chest so tightly I thought I might die. I ran, bare feet slapping against cold floors, my stuffed Pluto doll pressed to my chest, down the hallway where the darkness stretched long and hungry.

I reached my parents' door and shoved it open, desperate for the warmth of their voices, the safety of their arms. Instead: a groan. A sigh. The rustle of sheets.

"What is it now?"

My voice shrank. I already knew the answer didn't matter.

The dream. The monster. The beast under the bed, it was all in my head.

That's what they always said. But that didn't make it less real.

I stood there, toes curling into the shag carpet, throat burning.

"I had a nightmare."

A pause.

"Go back to bed."

The words dropped like a stone in my chest.

No arms reaching for me. No voice to say, *You're safe.*

Just me, standing in the doorway.

Eventually, my father would relent, shuffling out of bed to sleep in my room, while I crawled in beside my mother, who barely moved before rolling over.

And so, I learned to fear it.

Not just the dark of my childhood bedroom, but the silence. The emptiness.

The spaces where I was left alone with the things that frightened me.

At some point, don't we all learn to fear the dark?

Not just the darkness in a room or the shadows under the bed, but the kind that lives within—the unknown, the unseen, the unspoken. You learn that not everything hidden is safe. The uncomfortable stillness that follows disappointment. The absence in places that should be filled with warmth. The uncertainty of what waits in what you can't yet see. Over time, you begin to equate light with safety and darkness with threat.

From that fear of the dark comes something more insidious: avoidance.
You may not call it that. You just need relief.
Something—*anything*—to hold back the dark.
A hallway lamp. A bathroom nightlight.
The pale blue glow from the living room spilling down the hall.
Whatever will push the shadows back.

The eerie quiet becomes unbearable, an abyss too deep to fall into.
So you fill it. A radio humming in the background. The whir of a fan.
The murmur of a TV you're not even watching.
Distraction becomes your shield.
If you stay busy, you don't have to feel.
If you fill the void, you don't have to hear what lives inside you.

Does this resonate?

You don't know it at the time, but that's the moment you begin disconnecting.
The point at which you start exiling the parts of yourself that live in the dark.
Because if you can't sit in the dark, you can't sit with yourself.

When you run from discomfort, you run from the very places where truth waits.
Truths like:
I'm more exhausted than I let on.
I've built my life around being needed, not truly known.
I'm still hurting in places I never let anyone see.
I just want to be loved.

They don't rise up to punish you.
They rise to free you.

But still, you may run, chasing sound, chaos, and connection.
Even after the monsters disappear, you're still afraid of the dark, not because of what's out there, but because you haven't yet learned what lives within you.

What you may not know yet is that the dark is also where you dream. It's where seeds take root, where transformation begins, and where truth waits patiently to be reclaimed. It's where the womb nurtures new life, where rest restores what's been worn thin, and where stars remind you that beauty still exists even in the blackest sky.

To move through the dark, you must start listening, not to the noise around you, but to the wiser voice within.

THE INNER VOICE OF WISDOM

I had always struggled to trust my decisions, especially when they affected others or threatened my ability to be liked. Again and again, I ignored the pull of intuition when something didn't feel right. I spent years bending, shifting, and contorting myself to fit what others wanted or needed me to be. I pushed aside my own inner knowing in favor of the voices around me, believing that my parents, friends, teachers, boyfriends, and mentors knew better than I did.

I thought my job was to please them, even when it meant betraying myself. I feared making mistakes, disappointing people, or facing conflict. More than anything, I didn't want to be seen as someone who didn't know what they were doing. So I pushed my instincts aside, convinced that others held the answers I couldn't find in myself. In truth, the whisper I ignored was the deepest part of me trying to speak.

That whisper is inside you, too, discerning and all-knowing. It is the thread that connects you to Source, the divine intelligence from which all things are birthed. This inner guide does not shout. It does not demand. It simply knows. It carries the wisdom of every lifetime, every lesson, every truth you have ever needed. It is the compass set deep within your soul, always pointing you home, to who you were before the world took hold and wounded you.

But you bury it beneath the clamor around you, under the weight of expectation and the shadows of fear. You silence it because its messages often require you to do difficult things—things that shake you loose from comfort, illusion, and attachment. Sometimes it tells you to say no when others expect yes. Sometimes it asks you to walk away when staying feels safer. Sometimes it urges you to leap into the unknown when every fiber of your being clings to what is familiar.

Yet what if this inner compass is not here to strip you of all protection and comfort, but to guide you toward what is most true and important? What if it holds the blueprint of your purpose, joy, and highest unfolding?

This guidance does not speak in fear, nor does it bow to doubt. It speaks in faith and in trust. It knows the path ahead, even when you do not. It does not measure time the way you do, nor does it fret over details. It simply nudges you forward, step by step, toward your most aligned life.

And still, you resist. You get busy. Distracted. Addicted to motion and the collective lies. You fill every empty space—scrolling, working, worrying—until quiet itself feels unbearable. In that restlessness, you spin narratives of doubt and uncertainty, convincing yourself you are lost and confused. But clarity was never outside of you. It was only waiting for your acknowledgement.

This voice does not chase. It does not beg to be heard. It simply lingers, patient and clear, until you turn inward and choose intention over distraction, presence over commotion.

But before I could truly hear it, I had to sit in the raw unease of silence, the kind that makes your skin crawl. It wasn't peaceful at first; it was deafening with everything I had tried not to feel.

Yet what began as unbearable slowly softened into an opening, a doorway into something deeper. I didn't know it existed until I stepped away from the frantic hum of the world and into the quiet of the wild. I remember sitting alone on a mountain summit in the Smoky Mountains, the sky stretching wide and endless above me. The valley below looked impossibly small, and for the first time in what felt like years, so did the chatter inside my head. There were no obligations, no emails to respond to, just the essence of my own being.

Every unhealed hurt rose like fog around me.
There was nowhere to run.
The mountain didn't offer escape.
It offered reflection.

And in the expansiveness of that mountaintop, with nothing left to distract or defend me, I finally heard it, that faithful voice I had forgotten was mine.

THE GUIDE BESIDE ME

From the moment I saw her, I knew Grace was more than just a dog. She stayed with me through the darkest stretches, guiding me across the rugged landscapes around me and the wilderness within.

She was my home. A steady force who walked beside me when the world felt too loud, too uncertain, or too heavy. She always led me back to what was real. Grace lived in the present. No regret for yesterday. No worry for tomorrow. Just the warm air, the earth beneath her paws, the scent of something unseen carried on the wind. She showed me that this was enough. That the next step would come, whether I planned it or not.

She taught me how to listen, not just with my ears, but with my body, breath, and spirit. She trusted the path, even when I couldn't. She never questioned our place in the world, she simply walked. And so, I followed. She never left my side. Not when grief stole my breath. Not as loneliness crept into the spaces I longed for someone else to fill. Not even when doubt told me I was lost. In those moments, she leaned into me—warm, steady—offering comfort to my sadness, as if to say: *I'm here. You're not alone.*

She knew love better than I ever have. She gave it freely, without condition or hesitation. No part of me—struggling, messy, uncertain—was unworthy of her devotion. With her, nothing within me was unwelcome. Everything belonged.

And in her, I saw something greater, an embodiment of grace itself. Grace that arrives even when resisted. Grace that never demands I be better or more worthy. Grace that simply comes, again and again, whispering: *You are held. You are enough. You are already home.*

With that grace came joy. Not the kind tied to achievement or fleeting moments of pleasure. Not the kind you chase, but the kind you notice. The kind woven into everything, hidden in plain sight.

She greeted each morning like a gift, tail wagging, eyes bright, already alive to the wonder of just being. She found delight in the smallest things: a rustling leaf, a cool stream, the sun warming her fur. Nothing was too ordinary to be sacred.

Through her, I began to understand: happiness doesn't arrive when life is perfect. It comes when we slow down enough to feel it. In the rhythm of the wind. In the comfort of a good friend. In the way life continues to move forward, even after heartbreak.

She brought me back to the moment.
This breath.
This body.
This life.

And when I tangled myself in overthinking, complicating what was meant to be simple, she showed me: life is not as hard as you make it. Eat when you're hungry. Rest when you're tired. Move when the path calls. Love, even when it is scary. And above all, notice the gratitude and wonder that is always here.

She was, in every way, a guide. A soul wrapped in fur. A wisdom beyond words.

Dear Fellow Journeyer,

There comes a moment on the path, often when the road is uncertain or the night is long, when you begin to notice you're not as alone as you once believed.

The world grows still enough for you to hear something deeper. A sigh in the wind. A fluttering in the heart. A sense that someone—or something—is walking beside you. These are your guides. They may not look the way you imagined, but they are here. They always have been.

Some arrive in human form: mentors, teachers, and soul-friends who reflect your light when you forget how to shine. They offer insight at just the right moment, ask the question that cracks you open, or walk with you through a storm so you don't have to do it alone.

Some come from beyond the veil. Your ancestors, those who lived, struggled, and loved before you, speak through your instincts and dreams. They appear in symbols, in stories, in the strength that rises in your core when you need it most. Whether you know their names or not, their presence is real. They walk with you. They guide with eternal eyes.

Spirit guides may take the shape of animals, elements, or energies that ripple through your days with uncanny timing. A deer that crosses your path in a moment of grief. A feather left on the trail. A crow calling out just as you speak your truth. They remind you the Earth is alive with messages, for those willing to listen.

And then, there are the quietest guides of all: the ones within.

The child within you who knows how to feel, to play, to wonder. You might catch a glimpse of them in magical moments, laughing too loud at something silly, dancing in the kitchen without thinking, or tearing up at a breathtaking sunset. They may have been buried beneath years of holding it together, of trying to survive, but they're still there, just beneath the surface.

Maybe it's the version of you who built entire worlds out of mud and sticks. Who sang to animals, believed in magic, or asked "why" a hundred times—not to be difficult, but because you genuinely wanted to understand. That child didn't disappear. They were simply tucked away, waiting for you to return, not with shame or judgment, but with curiosity and open arms.

The shadow holds the feelings and experiences you suppressed to cope with childhood's challenges, the parts of you that you thought you had to hide in order to be loved. Yet within the shadow lives deep, embodied knowing, the kind you can't access through the persona. It's not just a collection of flaws or darkness; it's a vault where you've hidden what you were told was too much, too sensitive, too angry, too needy, too different. It's where your unmet needs, unspoken truths, and untapped power live.

When you turn toward the shadow instead of away, you stop abandoning yourself. You begin to reclaim the parts you disowned to belong or survive: the voice you silenced, the desires you diminished, the anger you swallowed, the creativity you shamed, the needs you labeled as weakness.

This is the key to wholeness, not fixing or perfecting yourself, but remembering and reintegrating what you left behind. Because every part of you, especially the ones you've exiled, holds a piece of the wisdom you need to reclaim your essence and return to who you truly are.

Your future self is also a guide, one who calls you forward with steady knowing. They've already seen where you're headed on this path of awakening. And now they walk back toward you, arms open, ready to lead you there.

The voice of wisdom within you is spacious and clear. It may retreat beneath the noise of fear, conditioning, or past pain, but it never disappears.

Sometimes that wisdom arrives through unexpected messengers, even those who have hurt you. Those who triggered you revealed your unhealed wounds. Those who left mirrored your own self-abandonment. Those who opposed you taught you how to stand in your truth. Their absence illuminated unmet needs. Their betrayal awakened your boundaries. They were never the destination. They pointed the way, to the places within you asking for reclamation.

Every step of the journey has brought you into relationship with some kind of guide. Even when you didn't know what you were searching for, they were there to help you in your souls yearning for home.

The path is full of insight.
You are surrounded.
And you are being led.

TRAIL WISDOM

HONOR YOUR GUIDANCE

Not all wisdom comes with words.

Some wisdom arrives as instinct, silence, or a sudden knowing.
Your guides may not look how you expect, they may come as a stranger, a storm, or a still moment.

Sometimes they live in your bones, the messages of your ancestors, your inner voice, or the teachers who walk beside you, seen and unseen. To walk with discernment, you must listen more than speak, trust more than doubt, and follow the quiet pull of your soul.

ENTER THE PATH

Take a deep breath.

Imagine you are standing at the edge of a winding trail, nestled deep within the forest. A thick mist rolls across the ground, curling around your feet, stretching toward the place where the path disappears into the woods. The air is cool and damp, carrying the scent of sodden earth and the energy of something new. The trees around you stand tall and quiet, their silhouettes softened by a silvery veil, their branches reaching out like unseen hands, gently guiding you forward.

You can't see where the path leads, only the first few steps ahead. A ripple of uncertainty rises in your chest, but alongside it—something else. A flutter. A pulse of anticipation humming beneath your ribs.

This is the moment.
The moment where the old falls away and the new begins.

As you walk, the ground feels solid beneath your feet, but the morning haze dances at your ankles, rising and shifting with each step, making the way feel both enlivening and disorienting. The air pulses with possibility, hinting that something is coming, though it stays just out of reach.

You pause.
You listen.
There is no turning back.

The wind moves through the trees, carrying messages—words you cannot yet understand, but feel deep in your cells. A mix of fear and anticipation coils in your belly. Your senses sharpen. Every sound—the snap of a twig, the distant call of a bird, the soft crunch of earth beneath your boots, pulls you into deeper presence.

Then, a glimmer of light catches your eye, a break ahead, faint but undeniable. Your heartbeat quickens. You don't know what lies beyond this stretch of trail, but you know this: the only way forward is through.

You inhale deeply, letting the cool air steady you.
The dark shroud doesn't part all at once.
It reveals itself step by step.

And so, you walk on.
Into the mist.
Into the unknown.

Into everything waiting for you beyond the edge of the familiar.

THE WISDOM OF THE PATH

Every path holds something to offer. Some arrive quietly, almost unnoticed. Others crash into your life like a hurricane tearing through a village, destroying everything you thought was secure. Whether you choose them or they choose you, each one brings a gift: direction, movement, meaning.

How you walk matters as much as the trail itself. It isn't only about progress, it's about how you show up for the journey. The path asks something of you: your presence, your courage, your willingness to be changed. When you travel with awareness, the terrain responds differently, moment by moment, breath by breath.

Beginning a new trail can feel like pressing your foot into untouched snow. There is a hush, a pause, as if the world itself inhales with you. The air is unfamiliar, intoxicating, like the edge of a season shifting. The ground feels alive beneath you, sensing whether you move with hesitation or intention. Each step sends a ripple through your body, awakening a deeper resonance, one encoded in your soul's divine blueprint.

And in that stillness, a question rises:
Are you willing to keep walking?

It takes courage to answer. To move when the horizon is blurred. To keep going when the next bend remains unseen. To trust only the quiet urging of your intuition. Not every stride will be clear. Not every day will feel like progress. Yet even in confusion, something within is shifting, realigning, preparing you for what comes next.

This is the essence of the journey, not the destination, but the choice to walk.
To meet the silence.
To enter the space between what has been and what is yet to come.
To trust that something—your inner fire, your guides seen and unseen, the hands of fate, or the inevitability of change—will carry you through.

Because the trail is not just a line on the map.
It is a mirror.
It shows you what you carry.
What you cling to.

What you are finally ready to release.

You cannot unlive the instant you commit to something larger than yourself. That single motion, no matter how small, is a portal. A declaration. A new chapter.

There are lessons you can only learn with dust on your boots and breath in your lungs. Some days you move with a steady rhythm. Other days you falter, crawl, or pause. But still, you walk. And in walking, you evolve.

Each step forward is an act of self-trust, a quiet vow that you are capable of more than you ever imagined. Because the only way to truly know yourself is to walk—into the mystery, into the unfolding story of who you are meant to be. To let the path teach you not only where you're headed, but where you've been, and who you are beneath the wounds, stories, and scars.

THE SEED OF INTENTION

Before any path unfolds beneath your feet, something must first awaken within you. The journey doesn't begin with a step, it begins earlier, quietly and internally, in the unseen space where desire stirs and direction begins to rise.

That inner shift, the willingness to move with intention, is what gives the path its power. It begins as something small, subtle, almost invisible, planted deep within you. Like a seed, it holds no proof of what it will become, only the potential waiting to emerge. It must break open in darkness, stretch its roots downward, and reach for the light, all without guarantee of how or when it will bloom.

Seeds are planted both consciously and unconsciously. When you attune to what is sparking within you, your actions carry clarity and grounded purpose. But when fear, pressure, or old conditioning plants the seed, you may unknowingly set out on a course that leads you away from the life you long for. Unconscious momentum still moves you, but often in circles, drawing you back to lessons not yet integrated.

To walk with purpose, you must step forward with discernment. An intention is not just a fleeting wish, it is the spark that shapes the path before it ever appears, a devotion that infuses meaning into each move you make. Unlike a goal, which is fixed on the map, this inner compass is a way of traveling. It is the energy you carry, the truth you anchor into, and the direction your soul leans when the way ahead is unclear.

Initiating the journey, especially when the outcome is unseen, is an act of faith. It is the decision to keep showing up, to nurture the dream, and to trust that what you cultivate will, in time, take form.

But what happens when you push forward without pausing to choose mindfully? When you act out of impulse, chasing whatever numbs the discomfort, running from fear instead of moving toward truth? You enter the wilderness blind. Without awareness, you don't claim the road, you drift into it, pulled by old wounds or unmet needs. Decisions made in haste often become detours, the kind littered with thorns you didn't see coming.

Yet when your yes is born of clarity, when your steps rise from deep desire rather than desperation, you become a co-creator of the pilgrimage. A choice rooted in truth carries a potency beyond what you can imagine. It aligns you with possibility itself, drawing synchronicities, insights, and opportunities to meet you along the way.

The way forward will not always be easy, but it will always be meaningful. As you step onto a new trail—whether of self-discovery, healing, creativity, or reinvention—ask yourself:
What am I planting?
What energy do I want to carry forward?
How will I choose to show up along the way?

Decisions are not rigid. They are not a final destination but a guiding current—fluid, adaptable, and alive. If something no longer feels aligned, if clarity deepens, if new awareness emerges, you can pivot. You are not bound to the first version of your vision. You are free to refine, redirect, and evolve as you grow.

True alignment does not come from forcing a path to fit, but from listening deeply and adjusting when the call within you shifts.

Let your intention be your compass.
Let it ground you when distractions rise.
Let it be the light you return to when doubt clouds your vision.
And when the road grows difficult, as all worthwhile ones do, your intention will remind you: You are here for a reason.

LAYING THE FOUNDATION

It's one thing to speak of intention; it's another to embody it. I learned this the moment I stood at the threshold of my own path, when the idea of change gave way to the reality of it.

Before I left for my journey, I knew I had to do more than pack a bag. I had to take an inventory of my heart.
What was truly mine to carry into this next chapter?
What was calling to be honored?
What would support my growth and alignment moving forward?

To honor that clarity, I created a simple ritual, something to anchor me in what mattered most. I didn't just send vague hopes into the wind, I named what I longed for. I wrote it down, gave it space. Each decision became a marker of resolve, a promise that I was ready to begin again. With every breath, every movement, I infused the journey with purpose, trusting that by walking with devotion, life would meet me with the lessons I was ready to receive.

I wasn't scattering wishes.
I was cultivating commitments.
I pledged to face my shadows and free myself from fear. I knew that if I didn't turn toward the parts of myself I had long hidden, they would continue to mold me in ways I didn't choose. Liberation wouldn't come from running, it would come from standing still.

I vowed to live a life of deep meaning and direction, not just to exist, but to be fully aligned with my spirit. For so long, I had followed the rules, chased approval, and shrunk myself to fit inside a self-imposed cage. But I was done living a life that felt dishonest or half-alive.
I wanted something real.
Something solid.
Something that felt like mine.

I envisioned a home immersed in nature, a place where I could breathe deeply. Where the land could hold me. Where I could listen to the wind moving through the trees and feel a quiet certainty beneath my feet. A place where I belonged, not because I owned it, but because my spirit felt at peace there.

I planted a vision for a vocation that fed my soul. Work that sparked light inside me rather than dimming it. I was no longer willing to sacrifice my well-being for productivity or success. My life's work had to be grounded in something deeper, something that gave life to others while also sustaining me.

I made a covenant with my body.
Not one shaped by control, comparison, or shame, but one rooted in reverence.
This body had carried me through every moment I thought I wouldn't survive. It needed more than judgment; it needed care.
So I promised to nourish it instead of neglecting it.
To listen instead of override.
To move, rest, and eat not from fear, but from love.

I planted a vow of clarity, the courage to ask hard questions:
Why am I here?
What did my soul come to do?
And how can I live in alignment with that truth?

No more pretending.
No more distractions.
Even if it meant unraveling everything I thought I was, I was ready to know myself fully.

I gave myself permission to grieve.
To feel what had never been felt.
To mourn what I did not receive as a child.
To tend the unmet needs that had long gone unspoken.

I was tired of carrying resentment, tired of letting old pain make choices for me. I couldn't rewrite the past, but I could stop letting it dictate my future. In grieving, I could make space for something new—lighter, freer, anchored in the life I was building, not the one I had lost.

I set down my fear of being alone and embraced solitude as something cherished.
Not loneliness.
Not exile.
But sanctuary, presence, and wholeness.

I chose to trust that I was enough.
That nothing outside of me was required to feel lovable.
I released the belief that my worth depended on being chosen.
Instead, I chose myself—fully, deeply, without hesitation.

And yes, I called in love. Not just any love, but conscious, soul-rooted love—curious, connected, and deep. Love not about fixing or filling, but about resting in wholeness, together.

These were my seeds.
Rich with potential.
I didn't know how or when they would blossom, but I trusted that they would, in their own time. Because I hadn't just wished for change. I had ignited it. I was willing to walk through the wilderness for it. To weather the storms. To meet myself in the raw, unguarded places where growth begins.

These were not just intentions.
They were declarations.
And I was ready to nurture them, wherever the road might lead.

I had laid the foundation. But it wasn't until I began moving forward that everything unlike what I had claimed rose to the surface. The moment I committed to a new way of being, the old patterns, fears, and doubts returned—asking if I truly meant it.

TREADING NEW GROUND

I knew my journey would demand great courage, that it would force me to face what I had buried time and time again. I was determined not to turn back, even if it meant walking straight into the fire of my own dread.

And the fear came quickly. Each crack of a twig, each rustle in the brush, sent my heart pounding. It felt as though danger lurked behind every tree, waiting for me to misstep.

But it wasn't just the threats outside of me, the risk of losing my way, the sudden appearance of a rundown pickup truck near the woods, the shadow of something unseen that made my stomach twist. It was something deeper. The trail awakened old, long-hidden terrors: fears of being alone, of being vulnerable, and of the monsters that once lived beneath my bed. As I was beginning to realize, they hadn't vanished at all, they had simply relocated to the forest and upgraded their hiding spots.

Even in the midst of beauty, the light filtering through the trees, the scent of pine, the cadence of my breath syncing with nature's pulse, a darkness within me colored everything as a potential hazard. My mind spiraled into worst-case scenarios. My mother's voice echoed in my head, filled with stories of serial killers and tragic news reports.

An abandoned cabin.
An unsettling glance from a passing hiker.
Footsteps too close behind me.
I convinced myself each one could be my end.

Some trails tested my endurance, pushing my body until I thought I might collapse. Others tried my patience, winding through endless switchbacks that left me questioning if I was getting anywhere at all. Still others confronted me with silence so deep there was nowhere to run from myself. And there were moments of surrender, when rain poured in sheets, rivers surged without mercy, and all I could do was trust the ground beneath me and the stubborn determination that kept me moving forward.

Each road broke me open in ways I never expected. With every step, I was learning to trust myself, to walk with fear rather than run from it, to breathe through uncertainty and keep going even when everything in me wanted to go home. The only way out was through, and the path was asking me to give everything I had. At times, I felt raw, stripped of the identities I once clung to, uncertain of who I was anymore. Even the wilderness seemed to mirror my own disorientation.

LOST IN THE WILDERNESS

One day on my journey, after trekking for hours through the dense woods of western Pennsylvania's Allegheny National Forest, I emerged at the edge of a river only to find the trail had vanished. Recent rains had turned the water into a relentless force, erasing any sign of a way forward. What had once been solid ground was now a mess of uprooted branches and scattered rocks.

I froze, a jolt of dread rippling through my body. The familiar path was gone. The trail markers, if they had ever been there, were buried beneath debris. None of the trees bore that white slash signaling I was still on course. I tried to recall the last turn, the last familiar bend, but the trees loomed in every direction—identical, indifferent. I kept walking, hoping movement itself would bring clarity, but each step only pulled me deeper into the wilderness.

The quiet pressed in from all sides, oppressive, almost claustrophobic, as if the forest itself were closing in. The fading sun slanted through the pines, shadows stretching long across the ground as daylight slipped away.

I was lost. Grace trotted beside me, her paws brushing softly against the forest floor. She sensed my fear, nudging my leg, grounding me for a moment with her faithful presence. When I hesitated, she circled back, tail wagging faintly, eyes meeting mine with quiet reassurance. But when I looked up, dusk had fallen. The trees blurred together, dissolving what little sense of direction I had left.

Food was low.
My water, nearly gone.
Panic clawed its way to the surface.
I tried to push it down, to remind myself I couldn't be far from where I'd started. But the truth was clear, I had no idea where I was.

A rustle in the trees. The sound sliced through the stillness. My body locked as something massive stirred. From the underbrush, a shape emerged—slow, deliberate, commanding. The air thickened, carrying something ancient, wild, untamed.

A black bear. Shoulders rolling with quiet power, dark fur rippling in the dim light. Its small eyes fixed on me—unreadable. My breathing went shallow. My heart pounded in my ears. The bear exhaled, a low, guttural breath I felt in my chest.

Not aggression.
A warning.
A reminder that I was in its world now.

My first thought was Grace. My pulse raced as I imagined her barking, lunging, or provoking. But instead, she did something remarkable. She lay down, eyes steady on the bear, body yielding to the moment in a way I had yet to learn. I followed her lead.

The bear sniffed the air, gaze drifting over me—calm, assessing. My fingers curled into fists, pressing into the damp soil. Then, with the unbothered ease of something that fears nothing, it turned and slipped back into the trees.

Gone.

Time slowed, though my body hadn't caught up, still gripped by disbelief, skin tingling with the residue of fear. Grace hadn't moved. She looked up at me—present, aware. I finally exhaled.

Then I prayed. Not with words, but with the exhausted surrender of someone who had nothing left to hold onto. I was lost, small, out of answers, left with only this moment, this dog, and whatever path still waited beyond the trees.

And then Grace stood. Without pause, she began to walk, not aimlessly, not uncertainly, but with intention. I held back for a beat, then followed. She moved as if she knew something I didn't, her pace steadfast and sure. We wove through the pines, the air cooling as the last light drained from the sky. My heartbeat slowed, falling into rhythm with the faint crackle of twigs and the soft padding of paws.

Then, as if the universe had been listening all along, we found it.

A sign.
A wooden post standing firm in the dirt.
The words carved into it were almost absurd in their simplicity:
TRAILHEAD PARKING AREA – 0.8 MILES

Relief hit me so hard my knees nearly gave out. A laugh, part disbelief, part gratitude, escaped my lips. Grace wagged her tail, just once, as if she'd known the ending all along. We were almost back.

Later I would realize what that moment had to teach me. Sometimes the path disappears. The signs vanish and fear takes hold. But stillness, trust, and instinct know the way. And when all else fails, a good dog—and a little grace—can carry you home.

The bear carried its own meaning. In many traditions, it is seen as a sacred totem: guide of the inner cave. Protector. Healer. Symbol of solitude and strength. The bear teaches you to turn inward, to listen for the wisdom found only in stillness, and to trust your own sense of direction, even when the way ahead is unclear.

I think the bear was preparing me all along.

Dear Fellow Journeyer,

Stepping onto the path is an act of courage.

Whether you're walking into the wild or into parts of yourself you've long avoided, it all begins the same way—with a feeling, a pull, a knowing that won't let you stay where you are.

As you take those first steps, carry with you the seeds of intention. Plant them with care, knowing some will root quickly while others will lie dormant, waiting for the right moment to grow. Trust that whatever you sow with honesty and heart will shape your journey in ways you cannot yet see.

But know this:
At some point, you will lose your way.
The markers will vanish.
The direction you were once so sure of will dissolve into uncertainty.
Fear will creep in.
Doubt will tell you that you've made a mistake.
This is part of the wilderness within, the place where the mind grasps for control and the heart is asked to surrender.

And surrender you must.
Not in defeat, but in trust.

Trust that being lost is part of the journey. Believe that what feels like an ending is often a call to shift your perspective, to listen more deeply. Know that the ground beneath you will hold you, even when you don't know where it leads.

The path reveals itself when it's ready, maybe in a moment of intuition, in the gentle prompting of something greater, or in the steady presence of a companion who knows the way when you do not.

One step at a time, you will find your way forward, not by force, but by faith.

So, walk on.
Not without fear, but with the courage to meet it.
Not without uncertainty, but with the willingness to be created by it.
And when you feel lost, remember, you are exactly where you are meant to be.

TRAIL WISDOM

EMBODY COURAGE

Courage isn't the absence of fear, it's choosing to move with your heart anyway.
Let it tremble. Let it ache.
Let the doubt sit beside you, but don't hand it the reins.
Take the step anyway.

Because courage lives in the doing.
Strength is built in the choosing.
And power is found in the truth you refuse to abandon, especially when it would
be easier to turn back.

Trust that discomfort can coexist with bravery.
Trust that your next step is enough.
And trust that on the other side of fear is a version of you who is so grateful you
didn't let fear win.

CHALLENGES AND TRIALS

Take a deep breath.

Imagine yourself standing at the base of a great mountain.
This is not just any mountain—it is your mountain.

A sacred journey.
A mirror for your own life.
It is filled with trials, obstacles, and triumphs.

Feel the solid dirt beneath your feet.
Let it hold, ground and support you.

Now, you take your first step.

The trail ahead is steep, winding, and unpredictable.
Some stretches are smooth and steady under your boots.
Others are rocky, uneven, and uncertain.

You feel a weight on your shoulders, a familiar weight. These are the burdens of what came before and what hasn't yet arrived: residual hurt, lingering fear, and the anxious anticipation of what might be, all tucked away in the backpack you carry.

Pause.
Breathe.
Inhale.
Exhale.

The trail begins to narrow. The wind picks up, howling through the trees like haunt-ings from the past—lessons learned, voices remembered, and challenges endured.

The trees sway, rooted and strong. You come to a river.
Cold, rushing water cuts across your path.
You pause. Fear stirs in your belly.
What if you can't cross?

But then—you listen.

The water isn't here to stop you.
It is here to teach you: flow, patience, and adaptability.
You find stepping stones beneath the surface.

One by one, you cross.
The cool water laps at your ankles, but it does not sweep you away.

You climb higher. The terrain grows rugged.
You stumble. You fall.
The earth is rough and unyielding—yet somehow, it still cradles you.

You are not broken.
You are simply learning.
You rise again, dust yourself off, and keep going.

The summit is still far ahead.
But now, you catch glimpses of the sky breaking open above you.
Storm clouds gather. Rain begins to fall, soft at first, then heavy.

The ground grows slick and muddy.
You hesitate, doubt creeping in.
Is it time to turn back?

You stop.
You close your eyes.
You breathe.

And you remember: Storms do not last forever.
You continue walking. The clouds begin to lift, and the sun breaks through, casting warm light across your path.

You are still climbing.
Still remembering.

And the mountain?
It rises to meet you.

BREAKING OPEN

Life has a way of breaking you open. The trials you face—heartbreak, loss, betrayal, the collapse of all you've built—can feel unbearable. They leave you exposed and uncertain, questioning your purpose, worth, and whether there is a greater force holding it all together.

From an early age, you're taught that life should be fair, that if you do the right things, you'll be spared the worst. But eventually you learn that pain isn't the exception; it is part of being human. None of us are immune. Hardship is the refining fire that reshapes you into someone you never imagined you could become.

Still, when you're in the midst of it, when grief closes in and the ground gives way, it's only natural to wonder: Why me? Why this? Why now? If God exists, why would He allow me to hurt?

But what if these aren't punishments?
What if they're initiations, meant to help you release the versions of yourself you've outgrown and step into something more real?

These seasons of loss don't just change your circumstances. They transform you. They reorder your values, dismantle the architecture of who you thought you were, and burn away false foundations so something truer can rise in their place.

To navigate the world, you learn to protect yourself. You build armor, a carefully crafted persona designed to earn acceptance, admiration, or at the very least, safety. It becomes the mask you wear, the role you play, the performance you perfect in order to belong. Layer by layer, it covers what feels too tender to reveal, your insecurities, your longings. Over time, the façade can grow so familiar that you mistake it for who you truly are, forgetting that it was constructed, not born.

And when the world doesn't meet you with kindness, when you're misjudged, dismissed, or hurt, you fortify that mask. You push your true self further underground, afraid that being fully seen might only lead to rejection.

And then heartbreak comes, the kind that doesn't just bruise but shatters. Suddenly, the persona begins to crack. You no longer have the strength or will to keep pretending. Exhaustion and grief seep through the fractures, dismantling the illusion of control you've held on to so tightly.

It's terrifying to feel the veil fall away. But it can also be a reorientation. Because beneath all the protecting and disguising is what's most real—something tender and profoundly human. In these moments of reckoning, you face a truth you've long resisted: Emotional honesty is not weakness; it is the birthplace of everything that matters.

Grief pulls you inward. It softens you. It draws you back to the parts of yourself you tried to abandon, and in doing so awakens a deeper strength, the bravery to be witnessed, even in your most unguarded state.

You spend much of life building defenses to keep hurt out. But eventually those defenses crumble, exposing what you thought you had to shield. Vulnerability can feel like standing in a storm without shelter. And yet, within that exposure lies your greatest power. It's where courage takes root, healing begins, and authentic connection is born.

What you often forget is that pain is what binds us. Beneath all that divides—identities, beliefs, and stories—is the shared experience of loss. Struggle levels the ground. It reminds us that we are not alone.

No, life isn't fair. But maybe fairness was never the point. Maybe what's important is how you respond, whether you allow adversity to harden you or to open you. Whether you let it mold you into someone bitter, or into someone wiser, more compassionate, and more alive.

You are not here to stay the same. Life will undo you, but it will also remake you. And in that remaking, you may finally meet the person you were created to be, not the version shaped by fear or illusion, but the holy essence of who you are when everything else has fallen away.

And when you begin to live from that place, when you stop hiding your sensitivity and start honoring it, you discover what you've been searching for all along: a sense of closeness. Not in control or pretense. But in the recognition that you are evolving alongside others. That behind every mask is a soul longing to be seen.

In these quiet, broken-open moments, a deeper awareness begins to emerge, a reminder that beyond the pain, beyond the stories and the characters you've embodied, an essential self is waiting to be reclaimed.

CRACKS IN THE FACADE

Over the years, I carefully crafted a persona—attractive, kind, courageous, intelligent, and grounded in strong values. I wanted to be liked, accepted, and remembered. So I became a master of people-pleasing, collecting achievements, contorting myself into who I thought others needed me to be.

I yearned to feel special. To matter.
Rejection felt unbearable, criticism like an open cut.
So I chased careers that fed my hunger for approval, roles that demanded talent, and a relentless drive to be exceptional.

On the outside, it looked like I had it all, success, confidence, a life that should have felt fulfilling. But inside, I was spiraling. Old wounds and unhealed trauma had taught me that vulnerability was dangerous. It wasn't just discomfort I feared, it was the possibility of being shattered. One crack in the image I'd built, and I believed the whole thing would fall apart.

Over time, the mask grew heavier, draining my energy, spirit, and sense of self. I was bone-weary, the kind of exhaustion that seeps into your cells and makes even the smallest decisions feel impossible.

And then, it stopped working. The praise that once energized me became unsatisfying. No matter how carefully I kept the image intact, anxiety, loneliness, grief, and doubt still found their way in. The harder I tried, the more I felt like a fraud, trapped in a life that no longer mirrored the self I was slowly trying to reclaim. The armor I had once worn for safety had hardened into a prison.

Deep inside, my body began to speak. At first, the signals were subtle—tight shoulders, clenched jaw, shallow breath. Soon they grew louder. My stomach twisted, refusing to digest what I had buried. Dark circles shadowed my eyes and inflammation flared. My immune system rebelled. Every symptom was a warning, my body's way of saying: *you're not okay.*

And I wasn't. The more I tried to control it, the more my body pushed back, pleading for me to stop suppressing, denying, pretending. It was asking me to listen. Not just to the discomfort. But to the wisdom beneath it.

Something within me was waking up, body and soul together, calling out to finally acknowledge what I had been dodging for years. The façade was never the whole story. Beneath it, an older, wiser force had been waiting, longing to be noticed.

It was the voice of the shadow.

THE CALL OF THE SHADOWS

Your shadow has been with you for a long time. It lingers in the quiet corners of your mind, carrying the scars of your broken heart. It has informed your choices, held you in patterns of protection, and influenced your beliefs, often without your awareness.

Born from the parts of you that once felt unsafe, unseen, or unworthy, this hidden self is made of everything you pushed away in order to survive. It holds your most tender places—suppressed emotions, inherited fears—imprinted deep within your being, woven into the fabric of who you are.

Yet you've likely been taught to distrust this part of yourself. In many cultures and traditions, the shadow has been misunderstood—cast as evil, dangerous, or wrong. You're told darkness must be avoided, rage silenced, grief swallowed, and anything unsettling fixed or hidden away. But those beliefs only deepen your disconnection. They keep you fragmented, turning you from the very aspects of yourself that most need your love.

Freedom begins when you welcome your shadow not as an enemy but as a long-lost guest. You are invited to witness it clearly, to feel its presence without shrinking back, and to begin an honest dialogue with the parts of yourself that have been reaching for your attention for years.

This is your summons into the wilderness within, to leave behind the familiar, the performing, and the appeasing, and step into the living mystery of your own unfolding. It is a sacred excavation, guiding you into the fragile, uncomfortable places you've carefully sealed away.

It asks you to release blame and take ownership, to open both heart and mind, to meet yourself with the same curiosity you so often extend to others. It requires a willingness to see clearly, to soften, to stay present with whatever arises. And perhaps most of all, it asks you to set down the mask you've worn to be accepted, so you can finally remember who you truly are.

Encountering your shadow is like walking through a hall of mirrors in a dimly lit room. Reflected back is not only the self you show others, but also the one who compromises to feel safe, lashes out in fear, or longs to be chosen but dreads being seen. It reveals the obscured terrain of your mind, your heart, your spirit—bringing into focus what you were never quite ready to acknowledge.

What rises from these depths is not meant to shame or diminish you. It is the echo of hidden desires, forgotten gifts, exiled parts, and unprocessed grief. This inner presence does not come to harm you; it comes to lead you inward, to initiate a deeper conversation with what you've left in the dark.

Often the first shadows to appear are doubt and fear. They rattle the foundations of belief, unravel certainty, and peel back layers of conditioning, asking you to question what you've been taught to accept as truth. To move through them, you must loosen your grip on what you think you know and meet the unknown with an open, curious heart.

As the path unfolds, this disowned guide may take the form of regret, shrouded in the heaviness of past choices and missed opportunities. It invites you to revisit mistakes, not to dwell in guilt, but to gather the lessons they carry. In that act of reclamation, regret shifts from a ghost that haunts you into a mentor who walks beside you.

Deeper still, you may descend into the valley of old traumas, where feelings long buried rise again. Once concealed as a means of survival, they now ask to be seen, felt, and released.

This unseen companion urges you to embrace your unarmored self, not as a flaw, but as the doorway to strength. And in surrender, the tears you shed become a cleansing river, washing away the stories you've outgrown, the silent agreements that kept you invisible, the anguish carried without words, and the costumes you were never meant to wear.

Each drop loosens the grip of what used to define you but now only holds you back. Pain, once feared, transforms into resilience, carrying you forward with clarity and depth.

Through this encounter, what once felt like a threat becomes an ally, a teacher and fierce truth-teller, guiding you into a fuller understanding of your own complexity. This journey is not about being consumed by shadow, but about learning to embrace the full spectrum of who you are. Wholeness isn't born from flawlessness but from integration, reclaiming every part of yourself with gentleness and compassion.

In the end, facing your shadows is a quest toward acceptance, growth, and freedom. It reveals that even within your most hidden places, there is the potential for profound illumination. And with that revelation comes your greatest power: the ability to rise into what has been waiting for you all along.

The call of my own shadow was no longer a faint whisper.
It had risen into a roar. And I could not look away—from the hurt, truth, or parts of me finally ready to come home.

MEETING MY SHADOW

I was in that strange and fragile season we call midlife when I left for my journey. Some call it a crisis—and sure, there were nights I cried into a bowl of ice cream at 1 a.m., Googling *what is my life purpose?*—but for me, it wasn't one dramatic collapse. It was a slow dismantling. One unraveling after another, each stripping away who I thought I was, until all that remained was a woman too weary to keep holding it together.

Everything felt empty. The world kept spinning, full of noise and momentum, while I moved through it like a dazed extra in someone else's movie—coffee cup in hand, pretending to look busy. I wasn't living so much as drifting, a spectator in the nosebleed section of a game I wasn't even interested in. I couldn't tell what inning it was, who was winning, or why I was still pretending to care.

There's something that happens in those middle years. A shift. A sense of urgency. You realize there are fewer years ahead than behind, and suddenly there's pressure to figure it all out before it's "too late." I wasn't happy with where I'd landed. Friends had attentive husbands, stable finances, kids who still called just to say hello. Comparison visited daily, taunting me with the image of turning sixty surrounded only by cats and a diet of ramen noodles.

Part of me felt damaged. I wondered what was wrong with me, that I hadn't found a husband to grow old with, or that I'd never had biological children. I had helped raise two wonderful stepkids for a time, but even that was complicated. My ex-husband reminded me more than once that blood was thicker than water, as if I needed that truth branded into my skin.

Now, with the window for children quietly closing, I felt like I should be grieving more. But I wasn't, not in the way I thought I should be. And that only deepened the shame, convincing me something inside was missing or miswired.
Was I heartless? Selfish?
The real kicker?
A part of me wasn't even sure I wanted kids.
And that made me feel even more broken.

Society would have a field day with someone like me: alone, childless, uncertain of

her next move. I could already see the headline—
"Breaking News: Woman Over Forty Still Has No Idea What She's Doing."

Growing up, I'd watched shows like *The Waltons* and *Little House on the Prairie*, captivated by the warmth and steadiness of those fictional families. I yearned to live on Walton Mountain, to sit around a table where love ran deeper than conflict. I wanted a father like Michael Landon's character—strong, tender, caring—and a sister like Melissa Gilbert, someone to laugh with and share life's ordinary magic.

Those stories planted something in me.
A vision of belonging.
Of home.

But that wasn't the story my family lived. Ours was marked by absence and resentment, where tension simmered and disagreements flared whenever we tried to gather. Eventually, we scattered, held together more by memory than presence.

So yes, I was lonely. Not just for companionship, but for something deeper—connection. I felt cut off from myself, from others, from the world around me. And it was on the trail, in the middle of nowhere, that I came face to face with that loneliness in a way I never had before.

By the time I reached the Cumberland Gap, I was already questioning the stories I'd been telling myself for too long. The Gap isn't just a place on a map—it's a historic pass carved into the Appalachian Mountains, where Kentucky, Tennessee, and Virginia meet. A crossing forged not by comfort but necessity. People didn't choose it because it was easy, they chose it because there was no other way forward. A passage carved by hardship, grit, and the will to keep going.

It felt like the right place for something to begin, or for everything to fall apart. I paused on the White Rocks Trail. The sky was heavy with low, unmoving clouds. Rain fell hard and steady. Mist wove itself through the trees like smoke rising from a campfire. And there, in that mystical stillness, I met my shadow in a whole new way.

Not as a monster lurking in dark corners of my psyche, but as a quiet presence that had been waiting—patiently, faithfully—for me to slow down and pause. It didn't rage or accuse. It didn't demand. It simply revealed itself, holding all I had cast aside: unprocessed grief, buried anger, and the panic that kept me frozen.

I sank onto a rock, exhausted, not just from the trail, but from years of holding everything in place. A tidal wave of emotion rose. For once, there was no television, no glass of wine, no slice of cake to numb the discomfort. There was nothing left to reach for but the pain that had followed me here, demanding to be felt.

So I let go.
I cried. I raged. I shook.
Until something within me broke open.

Decades of silence cracked, and feelings I'd long denied surged to the surface. Not just emotions, but memories. Every relationship, betrayal, and wound I thought I had buried emerged again—each with its own unfinished story.

Each release, every sob carried into the trees, every truth whispered into the wind, every belief surrendered, loosened the grip of what I'd locked inside: shame, guilt, sorrow. Slowly, they eased. They no longer needed to scream for my attention. They had been witnessed. And they were ready to be set down.

I knew there would be more.
More emotions. More unveiling.
But now I knew I could survive it.

For the first time, I understood why I had spent a lifetime avoiding discomfort, because facing the parts of me I had left behind felt like a kind of death.
Not a physical death, but a spiritual one.
The death of illusion.
The death of masks I wore to stay safe.
The death of stories I told myself about who I had to be.

It was a falling away of what was false—painful, disorienting, and strangely magical. It felt like standing naked in a storm, stripped of every identity I had clung to, unsure of who I was without them.

And it was okay. Because I wasn't alone.
There, in the messiness, I felt them—my guides.
My shadow, no longer an enemy but an ally.
And Grace—ever faithful, always near.

I didn't have to carry it all by myself anymore. Their presence wrapped around me like a warm blanket, and for the first time in years, I felt peace. Not the kind that comes from fixing or escaping, but the kind that comes from finally telling the truth.

And in that truth, I found not just the shadow.
I found my humanness.
My capacity to feel.
To fall apart.
To be remade.

I no longer feared the darkness within me, because in facing it, I found light.

And after breaking open, something else began to awaken. In the space grief had cleared, once the masks were laid down and the shadows welcomed, a new awareness emerged. Not the voice of my soul, but the one that had dictated how I survived.

The storyteller.

THE BIRTH OF THE STORYTELLER

Within the mind, where fleeting thoughts and hidden fears intertwine, lives a force that never truly fades: the inner storyteller.

We all have one. Shaped by your past, this inner narrator collects moments of failure, rejection, and disappointment. It weaves them into a script that defines how you see yourself and the world. Most often, it pulls from the shadow, focusing on what hurt you, where you went wrong, and how you didn't measure up. It feeds on old judgments, spoken or implied, and replays them as if they were undeniable truths.

But this narrator doesn't just remember what happened; it distorts and filters your experiences through the lens of old wounds. Pain becomes a pattern. Beliefs harden into reality, not because they're true, but because they're familiar.

From a young age, you may have developed a harsher version of this voice—relentless, shaming, and unforgiving. Its messages loop in the background, reinforced by situations that seem to prove them right. Without realizing it, you begin to seek out experiences that match these inner scripts. Well-worn pain, after all, can feel safer than the unknown. And in a strange way, proving the story "right" becomes a way to feel in control.

Over time, this narrative colors everything—your emotions, decisions, relationships, and even your dreams. It tells you what you can and cannot do, urging you to play it safe, avoid disappointment, and clip your own wings. The longer you listen, the more it becomes your default. You stop questioning its accuracy. You accept its messages as fact, even though they were never meant to define you.

As life grows more complex and uncertain, the voice grows louder. It analyzes every move, scrutinizes each decision, and pokes holes in your most hopeful desires. It thrives on doubt, amplifying your vulnerabilities and drowning out the quieter voices of truth, compassion, and clarity.

It doesn't just linger in the background, it starts to dictate how you live. It plants worst-case scenarios before you've even taken a step. It expects betrayal, prepares for disaster, and keeps you locked in hypervigilance. It's like being in a relationship that never lets you rest.

And let's be honest, sometimes it's downright histrionic. If someone takes too long to text back, it insists they must hate you—or worse, they're ghosting you on purpose. If you don't get invited to the party, clearly everyone created a secret group chat just to exclude you. If you speak up in a meeting, it swears you'll sound foolish and unqualified, and everyone will finally see you as a fraud. And if you get sick, forget a simple cold, it's obviously an incurable disease you diagnosed yourself with at 2 a.m. on WebMD.

The storyteller loves spectacle. It adds side characters, flashbacks, and entire seasons of content based on a single awkward grocery-store interaction.

When joy arrives, it warns it won't last. When serenity appears, it casts suspicion. It reminds you of everything that could go wrong, just in case. And when emotions rise, it stirs the pot, turning anger into blame, sadness into evidence-collecting, hurt into a courtroom demanding justice. Instead of letting emotion move through you, it keeps it alive far longer than necessary.

Eventually, the chaos becomes addictive. The stress, the noise, even the dopamine hits of familiar tension, you grow so accustomed to it that you forget what stillness even feels like.

But here's the truth:
You are not the storyteller.
You are the one who hears it.

Beneath the noise, underneath the fear and doubt, lives another part of you—
The one who watches.
The one who remembers peace.
The one who is not tangled in drama or distorted belief.
Your unstoried self.
Your higher self.
The one who waits patiently for your return.

Instead of believing the stories, begin turning toward the parts of you that keep feeding them. These wounded aspects don't need more judgment, they need your presence, recognition, and love. The more you suppress them, the louder the storyteller becomes. It will create as much distress as it takes to get your attention.

You have a choice. You can meet these parts with kindness, allow them to speak, and welcome them back into wholeness. Or you can continue to exile them, letting the script run your life.

Many people don't realize this choice exists. They spend years locked in inner conflict, mistaking the story for truth. But the truth is, there's been a doorway all along. The moment you become aware, everything changes. And from that realization, something new becomes possible.

Awareness cracks the shell, but it is only the beginning. To truly change, you must go deeper. The stories you tell yourself must be gently unraveled, rewoven, and reimagined, not to erase the past, but to reclaim the future.

TRUTH BEYOND THE TALE

I met my storyteller in a new way on the trail. Not as a concept. Not as a clever theory I'd underlined in some self-help book. But as a relentless narrator in my own mind, like it had downed six cups of coffee and refused to pause, let alone take a day off. It didn't ease me in. Oh no. It came in hot, spinning disasters with Oscar-worthy theatrics: *"You're probably going to twist your ankle and get bit by a rattlesnake. Alone. Because you're always alone. Also, everyone secretly hates you."*

It filled the silence with fears that hadn't happened but could. It replayed old conversations I'd worked hard to forget, dragged up past relationships like unwanted guests at a reunion, and kept anger simmering on a back burner I couldn't turn off.

Honestly, it was exhausting.
It told me I wasn't enough.
That I'd never be loved.
That people would always leave.
That I would die alone.

With no distractions—no phone, no work, no endless tasks—the chatter grew louder. It didn't shout. It slithered in, subtle and persistent, like fog thickening until the trail ahead disappeared. I hadn't realized how much space that voice occupied until the rest of the noise was gone.

One afternoon, while hiking a remote stretch of trail in Montana—tired, aching, and slightly over my own dramatic inner monologue, the storyteller really went for it. It scripted a future I hadn't asked for: lonely, unloved, and forgotten. My chest tightened. Breath shortened. It felt like being trapped in a movie I didn't want to watch but couldn't escape. And I was both the star *and* the audience.

But something awakened in me that day. Instead of fighting the voice or drowning it out, I did something different. I listened. Not in the usual way, passively believing every word, but with curiosity.

Where did this voice come from?
Whose tone did it carry?
What lived beneath all the fear?

I realized it wasn't an all-knowing judge. It was a survival script, a collection of old hurts and conditioned fears, building stories to protect me, even if they hurt me in the process.

So I started to talk back. Not with anger, but with awareness.
I hear you, but I'm choosing something else now.
I questioned the script instead of obeying it. And little by little, its tight hold loosened.

In that space, something opened, not in a dramatic, angels-singing kind of way, but in small, almost imperceptible shifts. Colors looked brighter. The wind no longer felt threatening—it was just wind. Even my protein bar tasted amazing.

I stopped bracing for the worst.
I stopped scanning for danger.
And for the first time in a long time, I was actually there, not in the future, not in recycled memory, but present, walking a forested trail in Montana.

That's when I saw the truth: the storyteller only has power with my participation. And I had been feeding it, with assumptions, judgments, and unexamined beliefs. Once I stopped jumping to conclusions and started asking for clarity, I noticed a difference. My relationships grew more intimate. I became more receptive. I trusted others a little more, and, even more importantly, I trusted myself.

I realized everyone around me has their own storyteller too. And maybe, just maybe, not everything was about me. The stories I'd clung to weren't true, but they weren't meaningless either. They were guideposts, pointing toward the places inside me that still needed tending.

In the end, healing wasn't about silencing the storyteller. It was about integrating it, letting it travel with me, without letting it choose the trail.

That relentless mind chatter still shows up sometimes. Of course it does. But now I meet it with a steadier gaze, a clearer heart. I know who I am beneath the noise. And that has made all the difference.

That's the gift of integration: when you stop trying to stifle the voice and instead learn to understand it, something magical occurs. The storyteller begins to transform. It no longer spins tales to protect you from pain, it starts creating stories that help you, and others, heal.

STORIES THAT HEAL

Once you stop running from your stories and let them belong, they reveal their medicine. In circles and conversations, across pages and firelight, I've seen how a single honest tale can soften a room, disarm a heart, and offer the kind of comfort no advice ever could.

Stories don't demand solutions.
They offer resonance.
And in that resonance, you feel seen and understood.

I've witnessed this again and again, in my own life and in the lives of those I've walked beside. Narratives that once carried sorrow or shame now serve as lifelines, torches, and mirrors. They become living proof of our capacity to mend, grow, and flourish. They don't erase the hurt, but they offer a way to carry it differently. They transmute adversity into resilience, and pain becomes wisdom.

This voice, the one that rises from wholeness, not fear, is different from the shadow storyteller that loops judgment, doubt, and shame in the background of your mind. The healing voice doesn't trap you in old patterns; it alchemizes them. It honors the hurt, but it doesn't glorify the suffering. It seeks meaning, not control.

Within the threads of lived experience lies a gift:
the restorative power of expression.
Each word becomes a balm.
Each account, a bridge, connecting hearts through empathy and compassion.

When you reveal your heartbreak, you loosen the silence that holds others captive. When you name your resilience, you light the way for someone stumbling in the dark. Shared vulnerability becomes a guidepost, reminding us we're not alone. In my own hardest seasons, when the journey felt unbearable, I held onto one truth: that my story, too, might one day become a beacon for someone else. That hope kept me walking when everything in me wanted to stop.

The difference lies in how you relate to your experiences. When you believe them without reflection, you become entangled in shadow. But when you pause, listen deeply, and make room for something new, a gentler voice begins to emerge.

You nourish this voice by responding with curiosity instead of criticism, with kindness instead of shame. You strengthen it by telling your stories in safe spaces, by writing them down, speaking them aloud, not to relive the past, but to reclaim it. Through expression, your experiences awaken something greater. One act of courage inspires another. And in the great tapestry of being human, the mending of one heart ripples outward.

When you tell the truth about who you are and where you've been, you create sacred space—not just for healing, but for belonging.

For a long time, I tried to suppress my own story. I thought if I just kept moving, I could leave it behind. But the wilderness had other plans. It slowed me down long enough to listen.

You don't have to wait for the wilderness to stop you. Your story is waiting to be heard—first by you, and then by those who need it most. Somewhere, someone is searching for the very words you've been afraid to speak.

Let your story rise.
Let it become the light you once needed.

Dear Fellow Journeyer,

I see the weight you carry, the silent battles you fight, the emotions that loom like shadows in the night. I know the exhaustion of holding yourself together—of wearing the mask so well that even you start to believe it.

The facade you create to survive can slowly become a cage.

You present a version of yourself that feels acceptable—strong, untouchable. You wear it like armor, hoping it will shield you from pain, rejection, and judgment. But beneath it lies the truth: the raw, vulnerable, beautifully messy parts you've been taught to hide, the parts you fear make you unworthy.

Eventually, the disguise becomes too heavy. The cracks begin to show. And the inner narratives you've clung to—of not being enough, of being too much, of being unlovable—start to suffocate you.

This is the moment you meet your shadow. And it's also when you begin to hear the voice of the storyteller. You know the one, it loops in your mind, casting doubt, spinning worst-case scenarios, scripting scenes of your inadequacy. It convinces you to stay hidden, to stay silent, to stay safe. It says, "Don't try. Don't speak. Don't hope. It will only hurt more." And over time, that voice can grow louder than your own inner knowing.

But here's what I want you to remember: You are not the mask. You are not the fear. And you are not the story you inherited. You are the one who witnesses. The one who can interrupt the cycle. The one who can choose a new way forward.

The parts you suppress are not here to shame you. They are keepers of everything you've tucked away, the unexpressed grief, the rage you swallowed, the fears you buried deep. They reflect the aspects of yourself you were never taught to hold with love.

Facing them is brave work.
Because it means seeing yourself fully, not just the light, but your darkness too.

For years, you repeat familiar patterns, avoiding, overworking, people-pleasing, shrinking, and pimping for love. You build a life around self-protection and call it safety. But in truth, you are simply trying to survive.

To step into wholeness, you must be willing to sit with what haunts you.
To remove the armor and meet what lives beneath.
To listen to what you've feared instead of running from it.
To question the limiting beliefs instead of obeying them.
To honor the ways you've coped—and then, gently, courageously, choose a different path.

This journey isn't easy.
It will ask you to feel what you've spent years numbing.
It will test your strength.
It will demand your honesty.
But it will also offer you freedom.

And on the other side of that work?
There is something waiting for you:
A life where you no longer have to hide.
A life where old wounds no longer define you.
A life where you can stand, unguarded and unmasked, and know, deep in your being, that you are whole, worthy, and enough, exactly as you are.

And when you arrive there, when you've looked your hidden self in the eye and rewritten the narratives that once held you captive, you'll discover something else, too:
Your voice. Not the one fueled by fear, but the one rooted in truth and love.
The voice that turns pain into wisdom.
The voice that reaches out and says to someone else: I see you.

Because your story, once a burden, becomes a bridge.
And through it, you help others find their way back home to themselves.

So, dear journeyer, keep walking and breathing.
Keep choosing yourself—again and again.
You are not alone in this.
And though the road may be steep, every step you take is bringing you closer to the truest, most liberated version of yourself.

TRAIL WISDOM

FIND YOUR VOICE

Your voice doesn't need to be loud—just true.
Whisper if you must, but let it come from the deepest part of you.
The world doesn't need perfect words, it needs real ones.

Drop the mask.
Let the truth rise like a song only you can sing.
That's your voice. That's your power.
And when you dare to use it, you give others permission to do the same.

THE WILDERNESS

Take a deep breath.

Imagine standing at the edge of a dense, untamed wilderness. The trees rise like wise witnesses, gnarled and towering, their canopy thick and shadowed. Twisted branches weave overhead, forming a barricade against the light. A heavy fog clings to the air, damp, unmoving, wrapping around your body like a worn, familiar cloak. The scent of decaying leaves fills your lungs—earthy, raw, alive.

Somewhere beneath it, something feral lurks just out of sight. A flutter of wings. The snap of a twig. You feel it in your bones—this place is watching. Listening. Waiting.

The way ahead isn't clear.
This is not just a forest.
This is the wilderness within, uncharted terrain of your mind, body and spirit.
Home to repressed emotions, old traumas, silenced truths, and wild wisdom rising beneath the surface.

And now, it calls you forward.

You begin.
The trail bends, leading you toward the dark mouth of a cave. Jagged stone arches above like clenched teeth. Cold air spills from its depths—metallic, acidic, like wet stone and rust.

You enter the Cave of Fear.
Inside, the walls shift with flickering shadows.
Your footsteps land soft and hollow.
Doubt gathers around you like mist:
What if I fail? What if I'm not enough? What if they were right about me?

Old wounds resurface—ghosts from your past, sharp as broken glass.
But this time, you stay.
You pause and feel the ground beneath you.
Take a deep inhale.
Lift your chin. Soften your shoulders. And say aloud:
"I see you. I hear you. But I am not yours to keep."

Up ahead, a faint light wavers—then steadies.

You move toward it. Step by step.
The cold begins to lift.

Darkness gives way to dawn.
You emerge, not fearless, but more courageous.
You have walked through fear, and it has not broken you.

Beyond the cave, the forest opens into a wide clearing.
At its center blazes a fire—wild, pulsing, crackling orange and gold.

This is the Fire of Anger.
You approach.

The heat dances across your skin—intense, but not destructive.
This fire does not wish to burn you. It wants to wake you.

You reach your hands toward the flames.
They don't scorch. They warm.

Anger rises—not in chaos, but in clarity.
Not to consume, but to energize.
Not to destroy, but to direct.

You breathe into the sacred fire.
You remember the moments you silenced your voice.
And you promise not to abandon it again.

You thank the fire and press on.
The trail winds deeper into the trees.

Ahead, a rush of water meets your ears.
You arrive at the River of Sadness.
Its waters move slow and wide, carrying recollections like fallen leaves—loss, longing,
the dreams that never took root.

You kneel by the current.
Your fingers skim the surface—cool, steady, vibrating with life.

Grief rises, unbidden.
You remember what you've lost.
Who you've missed.
The pain you denied just to keep going.

You let the tears come.
The river doesn't judge.
It simply flows.
It carries what you release, not to erase it, but to honor it.

When you rise, something inside you has relaxed.

You continue.
Soon, you come to a vast, silent gap—dark and wide.

Before you lies the Chasm of Guilt.
The trail tightens here, the ground dry and cracked beneath your feet.
The air presses in—heavy, stagnant, ladened with memory.
A stillness holds between the rocks, broken only by the rhythm of your own breath.

Regret lingers like a phantom at your back—reminders of words unsaid, choices you'd give anything to change.
It crouches beside you and taunts:
You don't deserve to move on.

But you do.
You inhale and step forward.
Then again.

The weight doesn't vanish—but it lifts, little by little.
The chasm doesn't pull you under.
It lets you pass.

As you move on, the forest closes in.
The earth turns soft, spongy beneath your feet.
Mist clings low to the ground.

You arrive at the Swamp of Shame.

The water is stagnant and dark, reflecting fractured versions of yourself—warped by judgment, failure, and fear.
They ripple with every breath, every thought.

Shame winds around your ankles, hissing:
"You are your worst mistake."

But you don't retreat.

You meet your own gaze.
And slowly, gently—you offer it compassion.

The reflection softens.
So do you.
The grip of shame begins to loosen.

You keep walking.

Around the next bend, you find them: rusted chains, coiled on the ground like sleeping serpents.

These are the Shackles of Doubt.
Forged from every voice that once told you:
"You can't. You shouldn't. You're not ready."

You kneel beside them.
They feel familiar.
Almost comforting.
But no longer true.

You reach into your pocket… and find a key.
You never needed to earn your freedom.
You only needed to remember you already had it.

You unlock the chains.
As they fall, you rise taller.

You have walked your wilderness.
You have stood in the Cave of Fear.
Felt the heat of the Fire of Anger.
Wept beside the River of Sadness.
Crossed the Chasm of Guilt.
Faced yourself in the Swamp of Shame.
And released the Shackles of Doubt.

And now, you understand—
These emotions were never enemies.
They were portals.
Each one held a lesson.
Each one pointed you back to your power.

You now stand at the center of your inner world.
The forest breathes with you.
The earth buzzes beneath your feet.

This is your wilderness.
It has never been here to break you.
It is here to reveal you.
To return you to one essential truth:

You were never lost.
And now, you know the way home.

EMOTIONS AS TEACHERS

Once I formally met my shadow, my emotions surged like a tide long held back. Their intensity rattled me. I feared that if I let them fully in, they would consume me, dragging me beneath the surface with no way back.

But resistance only gave them more power. The more I pushed away, the stronger they grew. I had opened a door I could no longer close. And as the carefully constructed walls I'd spent a lifetime building began to collapse, something unexpected appeared in the rubble.

She was there.
The most innocent part of me, the one always terrified of the dark, convinced monsters hid under her bed. A small, trembling girl, barefoot among the ruins of everything I had tried so hard to hold together. Her long blonde hair pulled back in a ponytail, her prettiest flowered dress paired with shiny patent leather shoes. She smiled at me cautiously, unsure if it was safe to finally be seen.

She was the part I had deserted long ago.
The one scolded for crying too loudly.
Shamed for needing too much.
Silenced by people who didn't know how to hold her pain.

And there, in that soul-stirring stillness, I did what no one had ever done for her. I saw her. I let her speak. With every tear that fell, I began to wash away the shame I'd learned to carry simply for feeling, for being alive, and for taking up space. She had been taught to fear her emotions, to numb and hide what made her human.

And as I looked at her, I knew she couldn't be the only one.
How have you learned to shrink this way?
To mute what hurts?
To dismiss what needed to be expressed?

From an early age, so many of us are told that feeling deeply is something to fix, not a strength to honor. You may have heard words like:
Stop crying or I'll give you something to cry about.
Don't be so dramatic.
You're too sensitive.

These phrases don't just pass through you, they embed. They become the rules you live by. So you learn to compartmentalize. You smile through pain, look strong while quietly unraveling, and tuck your sadness into hidden corners of your backpack so no one, not even you, can see.

But what if your feelings were never meant to be feared?
What if anger is not destruction but a boundary you were never allowed to set?
What if grief is not weakness but a longing to be acknowledged?
What if shame is not self-hatred but a quiet cry for compassion?

Over time, I began to see what I had missed: the emotions I'd pushed away weren't here to destroy me, they were here to guide me. They weren't threats. They were portals, each one leading inward to the tender, tangled chambers of my being.

And as I walked through them, something surprising happened.
Parts of me that had long been scattered began to return.

It wasn't dramatic or sudden. But little by little, the heaviness I'd carried began to lift, not because I had fixed everything, but because I had stopped turning away. In the quiet that followed, a different kind of clarity emerged. Not a vision of who I should be, but a remembrance of who I already was.

To reclaim yourself, I realized, you don't have to wage war on the past.
You have to unlearn the old rules.
You have to walk into the wilderness within—not to patch the cracks, but to remember what has always been true beneath them.

But as I kept listening, I uncovered something even more vulnerable. It wasn't only the heavy emotions I had exiled. I had also alienated love, joy, and trust. The very things I longed for most were the ones I had taught myself to live without.

In trying to protect myself from pain, I had shut out everything beautiful. And the cost of that protection revealed itself in unmistakable ways.
The light inside me dimmed.
I pulled away.
The spark of my inner child faded.
Life dulled.
The world grew muted.
And true connection slipped through my fingers like sand.

This is the hidden cost of self-abandonment: the slow erosion of your right to feel, connect, and live.

But the moment I stopped avoiding my feelings, something in me began to settle. The colors returned. I felt alive again. I experienced pleasure. And love, tender and real, landed in my chest. They had not disappeared. I had simply forgotten how to let them in.

My emotions became my greatest teachers.
Not curses, but beacons.
Not something to dismiss, but something to honor.
They guided me back to myself.

Of course, I had to ask—
Why had I pushed them away in the first place?
Where had I learned that feeling was dangerous?
That my needs were too much?
That sensitivity was a flaw?

The answers weren't only inside me. They lived in the air I breathed as a child, in words spoken and unspoken, in the systems I moved through, in the scarred adults who couldn't hold their own pain, let alone mine.

And I came to understand: my story was not an isolated one. These wounds are woven into the fabric of all our early lives. We are born innocent and whole. But over time, we're imprinted by the unhealed wounds and shadows of others. Our dependency makes us vulnerable, and we quickly learn to adapt to stay hidden, loved, or accepted. Protection often comes at the cost of expression.

To shield ourselves, we develop what I call traps and hazards—the subtle, often unconscious strategies we adopt to navigate a world that doesn't always meet us with safety or care. They begin as acts of survival. But over time, those same strategies can become cages, keeping us locked in fear.

You learn to deny your needs.
Suppress your emotions.
Bury your desires.
Choose comfort over truth.
Safety over authenticity.

Not because you are weak, but because you were taught your wholeness was too much. That asking for more made you a burden.

When faced with vulnerability, you retreat. You numb instead of heal. You drown it in substances, scroll past it on screens, bury it under to-do lists and endless striving. Some chase perfection, hoping it will earn them love. Others overextend, convinced busyness will outrun discomfort.

I've lived many of these patterns myself. But numbing always has a cost. What begins as a temporary refuge becomes a cycle: avoid, distract, deny—until you're no longer living, but merely existing in shades of gray. The same tools that muted unease eventually dull your joy.

Breaking free requires a radical shift:
Recognizing discomfort not as a black hole, but as a doorway.

Instead of running, you learn to stay.
To sit with what hurts.
To listen.

Creative expression, movement, breath, and self-care become pathways back to yourself. Genuine connection replaces the hollow chase for validation.

It means stepping outside the self-made cage and into the messy, unpredictable beauty of life. And in that messy, tender place, you begin to feel again.

This is the unshakable power of the evolutionary path:
As you are called higher, you are also called deeper.

You return to the same wounds, not because you failed, but because there is more truth, healing, and integration to be found.

This is where courage and commitment are needed most. Because no matter how much you've "healed," life circles back to the places still longing for your love. A subtle ache. A sharp reaction. A wave of emotion that catches you off guard.

These moments may feel inconvenient or confusing, but they're not accidents. They're sacred disruptions.

A SACRED DISRUPTION

Triggers reveal exactly what needs your attention. They aren't landmines, but portals, gateways into the deeper terrain of your emotional wilderness. Carrying old pain and hidden stories, they don't rise to punish you but to point you—sometimes gently, sometimes forcefully—toward the parts of yourself still waiting to be heard, honored, and held.

And yet, they often arrive with intensity—sudden, disorienting, and jarring.
A flash of anger.
A tightening in the chest.
A collapse into sadness that seems far bigger than the moment at hand.

But these reactions are never without purpose.
They don't create pain, they uncover where pain still lives.
They may look like present-moment responses, but they carry the weight of the past.

I know this intimately. There were days on my journey when solitude felt like freedom, expansive, even nourishing. But there were others when it unearthed something raw and uncomfortable just beneath the surface.

I remember one afternoon in Cuyahoga National Park. The sky was pale blue, the forest around me was calm. No crisis. No obvious reason to unravel. And yet, without warning, a tightness gathered in my stomach. It crept in like fog rolling across familiar ground. At first, I couldn't name it. But as I kept walking, it revealed itself, unresolved grief. The pain of rejection. The ache of invisibility. The longing for someone, anyone, to stay.

It rose in my throat like a wave threatening to pull me under. And beneath it was something deeper: a loneliness that didn't come from being alone on the trail, but from the part of me that had always felt different.

And just to make things worse, my inner narrator chimed in with her usual brand of "support": *Maybe it'll always feel this way.* Because obviously, what I needed in that moment was a side of existential dread. That thought nearly knocked the wind out of me.

It wasn't really about the trail at all. It was about the girl I once was, the one who performed, pleased, and shape-shifted just enough to be noticed. The one who smiled while her heart broke. The one who believed that if she worked hard enough to be good, lovable, needed, maybe then she wouldn't be left behind. She was still with me, buried beneath all the healing I'd done. And in that moment, her fear became mine again.

That's the thing about triggers. They don't always announce themselves. They slip into conversations and silences, into the hesitation before you speak or the rush to please. They live in the flinch, the clenched jaw, the breath held too tight. They are the body's way of saying: *There's still something here. Please don't turn away.*

For years, I tried to numb that discomfort.
When something hurt, I buried it in work.
I denied it with logic.
I smothered it with blame.

But on the trail, with no screens, no distractions, and no one else to pin it on, I had no choice but to face what was rising.

So I did.
I stopped.
The pain was insistent, and though my instinct was to keep walking, I had learned better by then.

I sat down, placed my hand gently over my heart, and instead of asking *Why am I feeling this?* I asked, *What part of me is asking to be seen?*

The answer came quickly.
The one who was taught she had to prove her worth.
The one who measured her value by how well she was liked.
The one who spent years waiting for someone to make her a priority.

So I spoke to her—not aloud, but inwardly—with fierce tenderness: *I see you. You don't have to earn your place here. I am so sorry.*

And something inside me relaxed.
The grief didn't vanish, but it loosened its grip.

In that moment, I understood: this was the gift within the trigger.
Beneath every reaction is a younger self still yearning for validation.

A buried story ready to be rewritten.
A hurt that no longer wants to stay hidden.

You don't need to fear these moments.
You need to slow down.
To breathe.
To listen with compassion rather than control.

If you meet these moments with curiosity instead of defensiveness, if you create space instead of shame, you begin to accept all of who you are.

That day on the trail, I didn't try to fix the feeling. I let it move through me and gave it room to speak. And in doing so, I gave something back to myself: a deeper layer of self-trust.

When I wiped the tears from my face, adjusted my pack, and began walking again, nothing around me had changed. But I had. Every feeling unearthed along that trail held a message, not just about my past, but about what it means to be human.

To truly reclaim yourself, you have to be willing to listen to what your emotions are trying to reveal.

THE CAVE OF FEAR

There is a cave we all dread to enter. Its entrance is dark and unwelcoming. As you approach, your throat tightens, your hands begin to sweat. The air grows heavy, damp, and unnervingly still. Light barely filters through. Each step sharpens your senses. The walls seem to close in, echoing your breath, your heartbeat, and your hesitation.

But this cave is not just a place, it's a feeling. A sensation that wraps itself around you and whispers, *Turn back.*

I know that cave well. It's where fear and I often end up, having another one of our long, complicated heart-to-heart conversations.

Out of all the emotions that have walked beside me, fear has logged the most miles. It has been my shadow, my sidekick, my unsolicited life coach, and occasionally, my uninvited houseguest who refuses to leave, even after I've clearly put on pajamas and turned off the lights.

To be honest, I don't remember a time without it. Before I had words, I knew unease. I felt it when I clutched the blankets tighter at night, afraid someone might take me from my bed. I carried it into the cafeteria, wondering if I'd be asked to sit with the cool kids.

It followed me into performing arts school, informing me that I didn't have what it takes to make it in New York or Hollywood.

In a strange way, fear has been my longest relationship. We've had our good times, our fights, and our tearful reunions. We've broken up at least a dozen times, only for me to find it sitting on the couch, sipping a martini and smoking a cigarette like nothing happened.

For years I wished it would just pack up and disappear. But over time I've come to see it differently, not as something to conquer or banish, but as something to understand. Fear never shows up without reason. It arrives when something matters. It steps in when something is shifting, opening, stretching—usually me.

Most of us are taught to run from fear. We numb it, override it, or try to reason our way out of it. We misread it constantly, mistaking old ghosts for present danger, or dismissing wise gut instincts as irrational anxiety. So we shove it into the shadows, hoping it will vanish if we stay endlessly busy, relentlessly positive, or perpetually "high-vibe." But fear doesn't disappear when ignored. It just gets sneakier.

On my journey, it revealed more than I ever expected. Sometimes it arrived as instinct, the subtle jolt that told me to change direction. Other times it challenged my need for control, asking me to trust a path I couldn't predict. And often, it sat shotgun with my inner storyteller, warning me—loudly—that I was destined to end up on *Dateline*, abducted in the woods and found in a dilapidated cabin, all because I took a solo hike.

Fear has a flair for the dramatic. But it also has wisdom. It says, *Pay attention. This doesn't feel right.* Like the moment you sense a red flag before there's any evidence. It's primal, fast, unapologetic—the kind of fear Grace responded to with a tilt of her head and a pause that made me listen with my whole body.

Other times, it shows up wearing a bad wig and last season's trauma, linking arms with your inner narrator and whispering, *You're going to mess this up. You're not that talented. Maybe just go back to bed until the world stops spinning.* That isn't intuition. It's a greatest hits reel from childhood, replaying old wounds in real time.

Still, I've learned to listen, not to obey, but to discern. I pause and ask: *Is this fear protecting me? Or is it trying to take me out?* That is the real work. Because fear has a standing reservation in that cave and always insists you join.

But here's the truth. The cave isn't punishment. It's a passage—a gritty, soul-stretching initiation. Navigating the dark isn't about being fearless. It's about becoming intimate with fear.

It's learning to tell the difference between the instinctual fear that protects you, the interpreted fear that repeats old stories, and the growth-based fear that signals expansion. Each has its place. One says danger. One says history. One says *this is your edge—lean in.*

So no, I don't try to silence fear anymore. I let it travel with me. I listen. I question. I breathe. And when I stand at the mouth of the cave again, and I will, I'll look fear in the eye and ask, *What are you here to show me this time?*

Fear may be my longest relationship. But these days, I'm the one setting the terms. At least most of the time.

THE FIRE OF ANGER

There was a moment on the trail I'll never forget.

It was day twenty-something—somewhere between *I've-lost-track* and *Is-this-what-transcendence-feels-like*—or maybe just dehydration. I was halfway up a steep incline, boots sinking into mud, mosquitos throwing a rave around my face, and my pack digging into that one exact spot on my shoulder that always screamed, *you're not built for this.* The trail was rocky, my sock was bunched, and my skin itched like crazy.

And then, I lost it.
Not in a graceful, enlightened way.
In a full-body, expletive-laced, hands-to-the-sky meltdown.

I screamed into the trees. Not a noble, primal goddess roar—no. This was more like an *"I hate everyone and everything"* epic unraveling. Birds scattered. Grace gave me side-eye. And I stood there, panting, red-faced, fists clenched, like a woman possessed.

But what possessed me wasn't just trail frustration. It was years of buried rage finally catching up to me. Anger doesn't ask permission. It kicks down the door, throws your book across the room, and says, *We need to talk.*

Anger is not polite. It is not quiet. And it sure as hell isn't comfortable. It's a fire. Not the marshmallow-roasting kind, this is a full-blown, soul-clearing inferno.

It begins in the body. For me, it rises hot in my chest, tight in my jaw, buzzing in my fingertips like they've forgotten how to hold back. The air feels electric. My voice sharpens. I snap quicker, react faster, and filter less.

For a long time, I feared that fire. I grew up believing anger was dangerous. I saw it explode and leave wreckage. I learned to tiptoe around it, smooth it over, avoid being the one who caused it, or worse, expressed it. I became a master of diplomacy, able to mediate a family feud while swallowing my own fury like it was my job.

Somewhere along the way, I got the message: *Good girls don't get angry. Respectable therapists definitely don't get angry. And if you want to be loved, keep it down and keep it together.* So I did. Until my body couldn't anymore.

That day on the trail wasn't a breakdown. It was a breakthrough. Because I wasn't mad about the incline or the bugs. I was mad about every time I said yes when I meant no. Every time I stayed silent when I wanted to scream. Every time I made someone else comfortable at the expense of my own needs.

That fire wasn't there to destroy me. It was there to wake me up.

Anger, I've learned, is a fierce teacher. It shows you where you've betrayed yourself. It illuminates your values, your boundaries, and your voice. It speaks when you've tolerated too much for too long. It rises when something important has been crossed. Not because there's anything wrong with you, but because something inside is finally saying: *Enough.*

Still, anger is often misunderstood.
You label it as immature, irrational, and dangerous.
You suppress it until it leaks sideways, through sarcasm, passive-aggression, or snippy one-liners that sting.
You smile with clenched teeth.
You talk about "letting it go" without ever letting it out.

But unexpressed rage doesn't disappear.
It metastasizes, into resentment, bitterness, exhaustion, and numbness. The longer you avoid it, the heavier it becomes. It calcifies, dims your spark, and slowly disconnects you from passion, vitality, and power.

When you meet anger with respect, though, when you breathe through it, listen to it, dance with it instead of fighting, it becomes a force for restoration. A fire that doesn't scorch but illuminates.

These days, when anger rises, I don't panic.
I pause.
I ask, *What do I need to know?*

Sometimes it says: *You're giving too much again.*
Sometimes it says: *You've crossed your own boundary.*
Sometimes it simply says: *Speak.*

And so I do. Not with destruction, but with clarity, conviction, and care.

Because anger, when integrated, becomes fuel.
It strengthens your backbone.
It fine-tunes your discernment.
It gives weight to your no and gravity to your yes.

So no, I don't fear my fire anymore.
I've learned to tend it, to trust it, to let it burn away what keeps me bound—without burning me out.

Anger is not your rival.
It is your compass.

And when it flares, don't run from it. Step in.
Because on the other side of that blaze... is you.
The *real* you.
Unapologetic.
Awake.
And absolutely on fire.

THE RIVER OF SADNESS

There's a spot I found on the trail in the Pisgah National Forest, tucked beyond a bend where the trees part just wide enough to let the sky breathe. A slow, silty stream wound its way through rock and root.

I stumbled upon it on a day I was particularly raw. I hadn't planned on stopping, but the waters called me in that subtle, soul-level way—the way grief does when you've been trying to outrun it for miles.

I dropped my pack, peeled off my boots and socks, and stepped into the cold rush, gasping as it swallowed my ankles. It was mountain-cold, startling, electric, and alive.

Grace, of course, had already made herself at home. She's always loved the water; honestly, I'm convinced she was a dolphin in another life. She bounded ahead and plunged in, immersing herself fully, lapping at the river with her long tongue, tail swishing, eyes bright with joy. This sanctuary belonged to her too.

I waded in more slowly, feeling the soft silt shift beneath my feet, the flow wrapping around my calves like a silken thread. Sunlight filtered through the canopy above, dancing across the surface in shimmering golds and silvers.

I crouched down and let the water slip through my fingers. Beneath me, smooth stones appeared in shades of moss green, clay red, and dusky blue. Some were flat and round like coins. Others jagged and unpolished, their edges softened only by years of passage. Fallen leaves drifted past, fragile vessels surrendering to the current. Even the air smelled different here, earthy and mineral-rich, like stone warmed by sun and time.

I hadn't meant to create a ritual, but that's what it became. I stood there, knee-deep, letting the stream circle around me. Then I reached down and picked up two stones, one in each hand, like sacred offerings. One for what I had lost. One for what I was still learning to navigate. I didn't speak aloud. I didn't need to. The river understood.

Rivers have always been silent witnesses to the ebb and flow of life. They carry the stories of generations, and in many traditions they are seen as symbols of collective sorrow, coursing with the tears of those who came before us. Each droplet carries emotion—pain, longing, loneliness, despair—blending into a single stream of grief.

That day, my sadness joined theirs. It began in my body, as it always does: a tightening in my chest, a lump in my throat, the sting of tears I tried, unsuccessfully, to blink away. For so long, I had believed grief would destroy me if I let it all the way in. I treated it as something to survive, not something to embody.

But grief doesn't want to be ignored.
It wants to be witnessed.

And standing in that river, I finally stopped resisting. I let it rise until I felt its chill in every part of me. I let it engulf me—emotionally, completely—let it undo me. And in doing so, I discovered: I didn't sink. I surfaced. Tired, changed, but still here.

Faces came to me, people and animals I had loved and lost. Memories surfaced like driftwood: promises broken, betrayals, words left unsaid, dreams I once imagined. The waters didn't demand I fix any of it. They simply asked me to feel.

I held the first stone tight in my palm and whispered a quiet prayer. Warm from my hand, heavy with meaning, it carried what I couldn't quite articulate—maybe goodbye, maybe thank you—and then I released it. For a moment it floated, then splashed beneath the surface, swallowed instantly by the surge. Tiny ripples spread outward, as if the sadness itself were making room.

The second stone was sharper, less willing to be held. I thought of the version of me who had carried that baggage for so long—tight-lipped, strong, pretending I was fine. I let her speak through my silence, and then I let that stone go too.

One by one, I reached into the river for other stones, each one carrying a fragment of grief, of sadness, of the parts of me that needed to let go. I offered them to the current, not to erase, but to acknowledge. To be taken by something older, wiser, and far more powerful than me.

When the last stone was gone, I stood still, hands empty, my heart not yet light but somehow less heavy. I thanked the river for holding me, for transmuting what I could not shoulder alone.

Grief, I realized, isn't here to steal joy. It's here to teach you to cherish it. It reveals the depth of your love and the tenderness of your humanity. It humbles you and opens you. It allows you to sit beside others in their pain, not with answers, but with compassion.

As a psychotherapist, pain became one of my greatest allies. Because I had stood in its depths, I could hold others as they stepped into their own. I learned to trust the process, that the water always moves. That sorrow, when honored, will eventually carry you to quieter shores.

Still, sadness is a teacher we try to silence. We hope it will fade with time. But unexpressed grief doesn't vanish, it festers. It turns into irritability, disconnection, and fatigue. It lives in the body and the hurting heart. It sneaks into relationships, dictating choices in ways you don't always understand.

Sometimes, you confuse letting go with forgetting. You hold tight to despair because it feels like the only thread still connecting you to what you lost. But healing isn't forgetting. It's remembering differently. It's carrying the love forward in new ways.

The river of sadness isn't only sorrow—it holds tenderness, memory, and longing. And when you block it, you block the very things that make you real.

So now, when grief comes, I go to the water, when I can.
I breathe.
I feel.
I remember.
I let the current move through me, not to take me under, but to set me free.

Because when the water settles, you are never quite who you were before.
You are someone who has loved deeply.
Someone who has let life break you open.
Someone who knows how to be with sadness without losing the light.

Grief doesn't take you away from life.
If you let it, it brings you back.

THE CHASM OF GUILT

If fear is a cave, anger a fire, and sadness a river, then guilt is a chasm—deep, wide, and somehow always appearing right beneath your feet at the worst possible time. One minute you're walking through life, feeling semi-okay about your choices, and the next, you remember that one thing you said (or didn't say) in 2005, and boom, straight into the pit you go.

It's not intense enough to kill you. Just enough to ruin your day, your week, or sometimes your life. And the thing about guilt? It doesn't crash in loudly. It tiptoes, pokes and haunts. Then it sets up camp behind your ribcage, rearranging the furniture of your nervous system like it owns the place.

There was a moment on the trail when guilt hit me square in the chest. Not the slow, creeping kind. The kind that tightens your throat and steals your breath before you even know why. I was sitting on a rock beside a clearing, sipping water and eating a soggy peanut butter and jelly sandwich, thinking I'd reached some kind of peace. I was proud of myself, honestly, proud that I'd finally managed to disconnect from the world for a while. That was new for me.

It felt like growth.
Like real progress.
The very thing you're told will help you find yourself.

It sounds wholesome in theory. Reverent, even. But as I sat there in that stillness, guilt crept in like it had just been waiting patiently for its turn.

The reality is, guilt had been with me long before that trail. It had followed me through years of relationships, telling me that silence was safer than honesty. I used to tell myself I was shielding the people I loved. That some confessions were too heavy to hand over and that withholding was far more compassionate.

But if I'm being really honest, I wasn't protecting them. I was guarding myself, from discomfort, conflict, and being seen as the one who caused pain. I didn't want to be called selfish or seen as a disappointment.

So I told partial truths.
I manipulated the edges of what I really meant.

I said just enough to not rock the boat, but never enough to be fully seen.

And in trying to avoid hurting others, I caused a different kind of pain:
The kind that comes from confusion and distance.
From only ever being given part of someone's truth.

There are people I loved who never got the full story. Not because I didn't care, but because I didn't know how to speak what I was holding. My intentions were good. I really believed I was doing the right thing. But underneath that belief was fear. And the longer I held it in, the more I felt like a coward.

It took me a long time to name it for what it was: self-protection. I wasn't avoiding honesty for their sake, I was avoiding it for mine. Because telling the truth would've meant letting go of the version of me they loved. It would have meant stepping into uncertainty. It could have cost me the people I loved. It meant risking being misunderstood.

And yet, not being transparent came with its own consequences. It kept me from being fully known. It kept me from the kind of love and intimacy I said I wanted. And it taught me—slowly, painfully—that silence isn't neutral. Withholding is a decision. And like all choices, it molds who we become.

That's the thing about guilt: it can masquerade as responsibility, when really, it's just perfectionism in a clever disguise.

Sometimes guilt serves you. It nudges you toward repair. It invites you to reflect, take accountability, apologize sincerely, and grow. Like the time I hurt someone, not out of malice, but out of fear. Seeing the pain on their face cracked something open in me. That guilt didn't shame me, it guided me. It whispered, "Hey, you missed the mark. Let's make it right." And when I let myself show up vulnerably and own it, healing happened. Between us and within me.

But not all guilt is helpful. Some of it is just… sticky. It loops in your mind. a highlight reel of regrets, always skipping to the worst part. And of course, your inner storyteller loves it—grabbing popcorn, dimming the lights, and hitting replay like it's hosting a shame-filled movie night.

I've carried that kind too. The guilt that has nothing to do with what I've done, and everything to do with who I thought I had to be. The "good daughter" who couldn't rescue her father from the grip of depression. The therapist who wasn't available 24/7—and still shoulders the weight of a life lost to suicide. The woman who said yes too often, and no too late.

This guilt isn't rooted in wrongdoing, it's rooted in the belief that my worth depends on never letting anyone down. Which is impossible. And yet, I clung to it like some kind of emotional insurance policy, as if suffering enough would buy back my redemption. Believing that carrying pain could somehow undo the past.

But guilt that doesn't lead to truth becomes toxic. It doesn't cleanse, it corrodes. It turns joy into heaviness, rest into laziness, and happiness into something you haven't earned yet. It kept me up at night, recycling old scripts:
You should've known better.
You should've done more.
You don't deserve to feel good when others are hurting.

Eventually, I started asking different questions. Is this guilt pointing me toward something I can repair? Or is it just replaying a story that is slowly trying to kill me? Is it truly mine? Or someone else's shame?

Because not all guilt belongs to you. Some of it is absorbed, projected or even inherited. Passed down through families, religions, and systems. You end up wearing it like a second skin.

There came a moment—several, actually—when I had to choose something different. To stop defining my goodness by how much I hurt, to release the guilt I had mistaken for a personality trait and to end the relentless apologizing for simply having needs, limits, or a pulse.

These days, I treat guilt like I treat every emotion: with curiosity, discernment, and boundaries. If it arises to guide me back into alignment, I listen. If it tries to shame me into self-abandonment, I challenge it.

Because guilt can be a mirror. But it can also be a trap. And I'm no longer interested in shrinking just to stay in someone's good graces... including my own inner narrator. She's officially been put on probation.

I still feel guilt, of course. I just don't let it rule my life. I check the facts. I repair where needed. And then I release the rest, like setting down that heavy pack I didn't even realize I was carrying.

Because healing guilt isn't about never making mistakes. It's about making room for your full humanity. You're allowed to mess up and still be worthy. You have the right to make amends and keep moving forward. Peace is yours, even when you've known pain.

Guilt may call you into deeper integrity. But it's not your forever home.

THE SWAMP OF SHAME

Welcome to the swamp. Not a charming, frog-filled fairy tale kind of swamp. No, I'm talking full-on, fog-thick, ankle-sucking, nightmare-in-a-storybook swamp—the kind that smells faintly of regret, mildew, and maybe that hookup you'd rather erase from memory. A place where time slows, where the air clings like a soggy sponge, and where every step forward drags you deeper into the quagmire of self-condemnation.

Shame isn't content to question what you did, it convinces you something is wrong with who you are. It nestles into your gut and mutters that you're too much, or not enough, or somehow both at once. It makes you want to disappear, not because of what you've done, but because you believe *you are what's wrong*.

If you've ever wandered this terrain, you know it's not a gentle hike.
It's a fight for your life.
It pulls.
It taunts.
It festers.

I've stumbled into that swamp more times than I'd like to admit. No warning, no cinematic buildup—just suddenly knee-deep in the muck, wondering how I got there. Again.

For me, shame showed up most around my body. It started, as so many shame stories do, on the elementary school playground, where tiny insecurities are born and then blown wildly out of proportion. That's where my best friend christened me with the nickname "Finger Toes." Yep. Finger. Toes. Apparently, my toes were a little too long for the neighborhood aesthetic. And honestly? They weren't wrong. My toes are expressive, let's just say if a piano were nearby, I could probably play a tune.

Then came the butt comments. "You've got a big butt," a well-meaning friend announced while backpacking through Europe. This was long before people were paying surgeons good money for the feature I wanted to disappear.

So I learned to flatten, shrink, tighten, and tame every inch of myself. But my stomach? She never played along. She kept her soft little curve like a quiet rebel refusing to be bullied into submission.

And then... menopause. I thought I'd made peace with my body until menopause waltzed in like a guest at a silent retreat—loud, unpredictable, as if someone inflated me with a bicycle pump and forgot to stop. My waist vanished, my moods staged a coup, and I found myself Googling things like, *"Is it normal to gain weight from thinking about carbs?"*

Here's the truth: I've had a complicated relationship with my body, even when it looked its "best." Even when I hiked 1,000 miles and weighed 103 pounds soaking wet—sun-kissed, trail-toned, and strong as hell. But this body is the only one I've got.

She has carried me through heartbreak and healing, through trails and therapy rooms, through meltdowns and breakthroughs. These thighs have climbed mountains. This belly has held gut instincts. These toes—yes, the finger ones—have kept me rooted to the earth. And if my stomach wants to puff out as I age? Fine. She's earned the space.

Because my shame story was never really about my body. It was about believing my worth depended on it looking a certain way. So yes—I've got finger toes, a J.Lo-adjacent butt, and a midsection more croissant than chiseled. And now my relationship with my body sounds more like this: *Thank you. I love you. Let's stay healthy.*

That's how shame works, it doesn't just poke at flaws, it builds a full-blown identity crisis. She's not subtle. She shows up like your inner narrator's older sister, clipboard in hand, ready to list all the reasons you'll never measure up. And once she wraps her fog around you, even kindness feels suspect. Compliments feel like charity, success feels fraudulent and love feels like a fluke.

You trip on a rock?
Shame sneers, "Clumsy. Pathetic."
You forget a meeting?
She purrs, "Irresponsible. No one will ever take you seriously."
You set a boundary?
She mutters, "Selfish. Who do you think you are?"

For years, I tried everything to quiet her.
I overachieved.

I over-gave.
I over-explained.
I shapeshifted into whatever version of me felt safest in the room.
On the outside, I looked polished and capable.
Inside, I was tap-dancing for my life.

Because shame doesn't just haunt the past. She hijacks the present.
And yet, shame isn't the ultimate villain. She's a signal. She points to the places you were silenced, the parts you believed you had to hide to belong.

The first time I let someone see those hidden parts, not the refined version, but the messy, insecure, still-wounded me, I braced for rejection.
They didn't flinch.
They leaned in.
They said, *"Me too."*

That's when I realized shame had been lying all along.

Because the antidote to shame is not silence.
It's sharing and connection.
It's someone else saying, *"That doesn't scare me. I see you. And I'm still here."*

Shame loses her grip when you name her. Not to everyone, not all the time. But to someone safe. Or even just to yourself—shared gently into the mirror at 2 a.m., hoodie on, eyes puffy, heating pad pressed to your lower back.

These days, I still stumble into the swamp.
But I don't set up camp there.
I don't build furniture and decorate.
I name what's happening.
I reach for my tools: truth-telling, acceptance, and self-compassion.
I remember that shame thrives in secrecy and shrivels in sunlight.
And I let my dog Grace lead the way.

Because she doesn't care if I've made a mess.
She doesn't balk at my fears.
She doesn't back away from my pain.
To her, I am everything.

So if you find yourself sinking in the swamp of shame, hear this:

You are not damaged.

You are not beyond repair.

You are not the worst thing you've ever done.

You are a human being doing the best you could with what you had.

You don't need to be flawless to be loved.

You don't need to earn your worth.

And you sure as hell don't need to apologize for your existence.

Because freedom isn't found in perfection.

It's found in being real.

THE SHACKLES OF DOUBT

I used to wonder why I kept repeating the same patterns, dating the same man in different clothes, sabotaging success with a spoonful of struggle, elbow-deep in effort while ease and flow flirted with everyone else.

Honestly, if self-doubt came with shackles, mine had tassels and a monogram. At first, you don't even realize you're wearing them. You keep walking—forward-ish— telling yourself you're fine. You're just being realistic. Just weighing your options. Just waiting for a sign. You call it wisdom, maturity, and strategic discernment.

But beneath all that well-reasoned hesitation, something quieter lingers:
What if I can't? What if I'm not who I think I am?
What if everyone finds out I've been faking it this whole time?

Doubt is sneaky like that.
It doesn't scream. It seeps.
Soft, rational, and courteous.
"Just trying to help," it says.
"Better safe than sorry," it coos.
And before you know it, you've spent five hours color-coordinating your sock drawer like your destiny depends on it.

I've been there. I experienced this many times on my journey. I'd read all those cool books about hiking the Appalachian and Pacific Crest trail. I wanted to be the warrior hiker who lived to tell their epic stories.
But what I heard instead was:
You sure you're cut out for this?
Maybe you bit off more than you can chew.
People like you don't finish things like this.

Ah yes, there she is, my wonderfully dramatic inner narrator. I named her Rachel. Rachel wears skinny jeans and a tastefully neutral sweater. She's got that "effort- less" messy bun that never actually looks messy, and she always smells faintly of overpriced essential oils. Her finger wags like she's conducting an orchestra of disapproval, her lips smack with the precision of someone who's been critiquing since birth. Her voice? A cross between Jane Fonda leading a motivational aerobics class and Linda Blair mid-exorcism. She means well. But she wears me out.

That's the thing about doubt, it rarely kicks down the door. More often it slips in disguised as humility, caution, or perfectionism. It sounds like:
I just need a little more time.
Maybe I should wait until I'm more qualified.
Let me tweak this one more time before I share it with the world.

But really? It's fear in a business suit.

For a long time, I let doubt lead. I waited to feel ready. I thought clarity would arrive like a lightning bolt. Instead, it came like mud—thick, slow, everywhere. Eventually I realized: waiting doesn't build confidence. Doing does.

So I started walking with doubt instead of waiting for it to leave. And every step gave me new evidence:
That I could handle discomfort.
That failure wasn't fatal.
That my voice wouldn't crack open the Earth in embarrassment.

The more I moved, the more I saw doubt wasn't trying to destroy me, it was trying to protect something tender. The part of me still clinging to old scripts:
That I wasn't good enough.
That I had to work harder than anyone else to succeed.
That I was getting too old for the dreams I once held as a little girl.

But those weren't truths. They were costumes I'd outgrown. And I was tired of auditioning for a role I never even wanted.

Because there's a cost to letting doubt decide. Not just in missed opportunities, but in missed versions of yourself.
The version that speaks up.
The one that risks.
The one that manifests like crazy.

And that cost? It's too damn high.

So I started asking different questions:
What is this fear protecting?
What am I really afraid will happen—and can I survive it?
What if I stop trying to eliminate doubt, and just stop giving it the mic?

I began to move differently.
Still scared. Still unsure.
But willing.

Because here's the truth no one tells you:
Readiness is a myth.
Clarity is usually retrospective.
And doubt doesn't vanish, it just loses its power when you stop mistaking it for reality.

These days, I still feel it.
When I try something new.
When I share something vulnerable (like writing this book).
When I step into a bigger version of myself.

Doubt still knocks.
But I don't answer.
I thank it for its concern.
I check in with the part of me that's scared.
And then I keep going.

Because I'd rather know what could happen than spend my life wondering.

So if you're waiting for certainty before you move, let me gently suggest:
It's not coming.
What's coming... is you.

More honest. More courageous.
More willing to try, even when your knees are buckling and your inner storyteller is doing jazz hands in the corner.

So let doubt come. Let it mutter. Let it flail.
But don't let it win.

Because the shackles?
They were never locked.

SHEDDING SKINS

When I set out on my journey, I thought I was walking toward something—clarity, maybe healing. But in truth, I was walking straight into the wilderness of my own shadow. The trail didn't just wind across miles of forest and ridge, it led directly into the places I had spent years trying not to feel.

I had become a master of emotional camouflage, keeping things light, minimizing pain, swallowing truths before they ever reached the surface. But the wilderness doesn't tolerate pretense. It stripped me bare. Every step uncovered another layer—fear, grief, and the old stories I thought I had buried for good.

Eventually, I reached a threshold, that moment when you either turn back or walk straight into the fire. The liminal edge where everything feels uncertain, and yet something deep within insists you keep going. There's a line from *The Shawshank Redemption* that says, "You either get busy living or get busy dying." That's exactly what it felt like, standing at the precipice of myself, choosing between collapse and reclamation.

The trail tested more than my endurance. It confronted my identity. It asked me to reevaluate everything—my past, my relationships, and my career. The choices I'd made to feel safe, and the ones I'd avoided out of fear. I had to face the guilt of disappointing others, the discomfort of never feeling enough, the terror of releasing the version of myself I had built just to survive.

And through it all, there was Grace. Literally—my dog, Grace. She walked beside me like the most loyal sage. When I couldn't find my way, she became my compass. When I was spiraling in self-doubt, she reminded me: life is still happening. She woke up every morning with wonder in her eyes and joy in her paws. She didn't ruminate on the past or obsess about the future. She didn't question her worth or apologize for her needs. She simply lived.

Some days, I kept going because she needed me to. Other days, I moved forward because she believed in the path, even when I didn't. She guided me without words—through presence, simplicity, and spirit.

The journey also taught me that healing isn't linear. It's not a staircase. It's a spiral, pulling you inward again and again, not to where you began, but to deeper layers of awareness. Messy. Untamed. Repetitive. And strangely beautiful. Like waves carving stone, the spiral wears away what's false and strengthens what's real.

At first, you awaken. Sometimes gently. Sometimes like being jolted out of a dream by a storm you never saw coming. You begin to see the patterns you couldn't see before, the ways you abandoned yourself, the stories you carried, the voice you silenced. It's disorienting, like opening your eyes to a life you hadn't realized you were sleepwalking through.

Then you rise. Not in a grand, cinematic way, but slowly—imperfectly—through each decision to speak with conviction, set the boundary, and feel what you once buried. This is where the real work begins. Where you stop looking outside yourself for answers and turn inward with radical honesty. Where you face discomfort instead of avoiding it, name patterns instead of denying them, and find the courage to act differently, even when it's hard. Rising isn't always graceful. Sometimes it looks like crawling. But it's still movement—toward wholeness, self-respect, and freedom.

And finally, you begin to embody. Not just knowing the truth, but living it. Trusting your inner wisdom. Honoring your body. Becoming someone who no longer betrays themselves in order to be loved. Integration doesn't polish you, it makes you more sincere, anchored and aligned. Your outer life begins to reflect your inner knowing. You speak with clarity, choose with intention and show up rooted in who you are, not who you think you have to be. And from this place, this grounded embodiment, you begin to lead.

Because your evolution doesn't ask you to become someone else. It asks you to shed the skins that were never truly yours. To return to the soulprint you came in with, before the world blurred its edges, and to meet that self again and again, with love.

Dear Fellow Journeyer,

If you're standing in the thick of your own emotional wilderness, know this, you're not alone. This journey—through fear, anger, sadness, guilt, shame, and doubt—isn't for the faint of heart. It will ask you to face the parts of yourself you've long avoided, to sit with emotions that feel unbearable, to surrender to the unknown. But if you're willing to walk this path, you'll discover something far greater than the pain you fear, you'll find yourself.

Fear will try to keep you hidden. It'll tell you that you're not ready, that the unknown is too risky, that stepping forward could cost you everything. But fear isn't here to stop you, it's here to speak. Listen closely, and you'll learn to discern between the fear that protects you and the fear that confines you. Step forward anyway. You are capable of more than you know.

Anger may rise like wildfire, intense and untamed. It is not your enemy. It's a signal, a fierce ally showing you where your boundaries were crossed, where your voice went silent, where change is long overdue. Don't bury it. Harness it. Let it point you to what matters.

Sadness will make each step heavier. It'll convince you that wholeness is out of reach. But grief is not a void, it's a current. Let it carry you. Let it show you how deeply you've loved, how much you've risked, and how alive you really are.

Guilt will try to trap you in the past, insisting that suffering is the price of redemption. But guilt only serves when it teaches. Beyond that, it's a prison. Forgive yourself. Keep the lesson and drop the weight.

Shame will tell you that you are wrong, not just your choices, but your very being. That if people really knew you, they'd walk away. But shame lies. You are not your worst moment. You are not the story someone else projected onto you. Come out of hiding. You are worthy of love and belonging, exactly as you are.

Doubt won't shout. It'll linger at the edges, always waiting to be consulted. It'll say: "Wait a little longer. Be more prepared. Be sure." But clarity doesn't come from waiting, it comes from walking. You've already survived storms that should've broken you. You're stronger than the voice that says you're not enough.

And remember, healing isn't linear, it's a spiral. You'll circle back to old wounds, not because you're flawed, but because you're stronger now. With every pass, you gain more presence, more power, and more truth. You are becoming, not someone new, but more fully yourself.

So walk forward, fellow journeyer. Even when the path disappears into mist. Even when your knees buckle. Even when you want to turn back. Keep going. The wilderness within you isn't your enemy, it's your initiation.

And as you walk, remember this:
You are not just facing your pain.
You are making space for your joy.
You are not just confronting your shadow.
You are stepping into greater love.

TRAIL WISDOM

LIVE YOUR TRUTH

The path will challenge you—not to break you, but to ask:
Are you ready to rise as who you truly are?

There will be moments when silence feels safer than honesty,
when blending in feels easier than being real.
But your truth was never meant to be buried.

It doesn't live out there, on someone else's map.
It lives within, in the wild places you were taught to avoid,
beneath the noise of expectation, beneath the stories that no longer fit.

When you choose to enter your own wilderness—
to sit with the shadows, to feel what you once silenced,
you don't just survive.
You remember.

NEW LIFE

Take a deep breath.

Feel the crisp, clean air fill your lungs, invigorating you with each inhale. The weight of the past begins to lift, dissolving like mist rising with the morning sun. You have travelled far to reach this moment—step by step, breath by breath, through discomfort and awakening, through uncertainty and transformation.

And now, you stand at the summit, a place where the sky stretches endlessly before you, where the sun carries glimmers of what could be.

As you turn to look behind you, you see the winding path that brought you here, every bend, every lesson, and every moment of struggle that molded your unfolding. There were times you doubted you could keep going and times the incline felt too steep. But you didn't stop. You kept moving. And now, here you are, at the crest of a journey that has rewritten you.

Ahead of you, the vast horizon opens, rolling hills, shimmering lakes, golden valleys stretching as far as your eyes can see. The world below is alive, waiting for you to step into it. You are not who you once were. The doubts that once anchored you have begun to lift and fade. You are lighter now.

The shadows that once loomed dissolve into memory, replaced by warm beams of sunlight lighting your way forward. Wildflowers bloom at your feet—vibrant bursts of color, signs of the growth taking root within you. You notice how effortlessly nature embraces change, how rivers carve new paths, how trees make room for new life, how every ending in this wilderness births a new beginning.

With each exhale, you release the burdens of old stories and the fears that no longer belong to you. The past is no longer a chain, it has become the fertile ground of your evolution. You are emerging—stronger, wiser, and more fully alive.

You place your hand over your heart, feeling the steady beat that has carried you through it all. You have arrived in this moment—fully present, fully ready.

Now, standing on this mountain summit, the world stretches wide around you—lowlands unfolding below, distant peaks lost in mist, the sky close enough to touch. Wind rushes past, cool and alive, carrying the scent of stone and possibility.

You pause, breathing in the promise of what's to come. As you exhale, you smile, feeling the warmth of the sun on your face, the solid ground beneath your feet. You linger in this peaceful moment, knowing the path will call you forward when it's time.

CLAIMING SELF-WORTH

After walking through the wilderness of fear, anger, grief, guilt, shame, and doubt—something began to settle. The intensity lessened, the inner noise quieted, and I began to see that healing wasn't only about releasing the past. It was about rebuilding, laying a foundation strong enough to carry me through future storms. And that foundation, I knew, had to begin with one essential truth: I matter.

I have something to say.

And I am worthy, regardless of what I have been through.

Before my journey, I didn't realize how often I had turned away from myself, subtly, repeatedly, in ways so familiar they slid beneath my awareness. I had built my value on approval and accomplishment, on being the dependable one who kept everyone comfortable, even when it required silencing my own needs. I believed that if I just gave more, proved more, became more, I would finally feel worthy. But the feeling never lasted. It flickered, then vanished. Always out of reach.

It wasn't until everything fell apart, and I stepped away from the monotony of daily life, that I finally stood in the truth inside my unraveling: self-worth was never something to earn. It was something to reclaim. It had always lived within me, buried beneath conditioning, perfectionism, and the belief that love was something I had to attain.

One evening, deep in the Smoky Mountains, after a long day of hiking rugged trails, I collapsed onto a patch of mossy earth near the edge of a quiet overlook. Grace lay beside me, her chest rising and falling with the fading heat of the day. Her ears twitched at the distant sounds of the forest, an owl calling, the rustle of wind through the trees, but she remained calm, entirely rooted in the moment.

The sun slid low, spilling molten light across the ridgelines, each one a softer blue than the last, dissolving into haze. Smoke from distant fires mingled with mountain mist, weaving ribbons of silver through the trees. I watched in silence as the wilderness revealed itself, not performing, not seeking approval, just being.

It was in that stillness, with Grace's warm body pressed against mine and the earth's quiet beauty all around, that I finally understood:

Nothing in nature questions its worth.
The trees do not wonder if they deserve the sun.
The rivers don't shrink back for not being oceans.
They simply are, and that is enough.
And so am I.
Not because I accomplished more. Not because I earned the right to be here.
But because I was *born* worthy.

That knowing didn't strike like lightning, it rose slowly, like steam off morning water. It had always been there, waiting to be remembered. And when I finally claimed it, everything recalibrated. I stopped asking permission to exist. I began honoring my energy, my time, and my truth. I stopped molding myself to fit someone else's expectations and began standing on my own.

Still, somewhere along the way, I had let life strip me of this awareness. I let the projections of other people's pain, shadows and judgment cloud the truth of who I am. Yes, I'd been hurt, but pain is not the measure of my value. I am the only one who gets to define my significance.

At first, the truth felt foreign. Doubt persisted: *You're being selfish. Who do you think you are?* But each time I chose myself, each time I listened to the wisdom rising beneath the noise, I reclaimed a piece of me.

Because self-worth isn't a single breakthrough.
It's a practice.
A commitment.
A daily remembering.

It shapes everything, how you love, how you speak, and how you move through the world. When you know your worth, you stop chasing people who can't see it. You stop trying to prove yourself in rooms you were never meant to be in. You start listening to your own voice over the endless distractions. You begin to walk differently, not to impress, but because you finally belong to yourself.

And yet, let's be honest, choosing your worth in today's world is not easy. Comparison is everywhere. You scroll through curated instagram reels and convince yourself you're behind, failing at things that don't even matter to you. I used to measure my value against people I hadn't spoken to in years, people who seemed to have it all figured out. Their confidence, love, and success made me question everything about myself.

Even jealousy, which I once judged harshly, revealed itself as a teacher. It wasn't proof I was lacking, it was a mirror, reflecting the desires I had long denied. When I envied someone's happiness, it meant I had forgotten how to access my own. When I envied their relationships, it showed me the connection I was craving but hadn't yet allowed myself to receive.

Jealousy wasn't something to suppress. It was something to listen to.
Not "Why do they have what I don't?"
But "What does this reveal about what I long for?"

The biggest barrier to my own self-respect wasn't comparison. It was the voice in my own head. My good ole storyteller had a PhD in overreaction, magnifying every flaw, turning every mistake into a verdict, and handing down a life sentence without parole. I believed things about myself I'd never say to another human being. I could look a friend in the eye and say, *"You are not defined by this. You are still enough."* But if I messed up? Clearly, it was proof I was unlovable, irredeemable and probably cursed.

I offered grace to everyone but myself. Worse, I clung to judgment like it was my job. I defended my limitations and argued for my unworthiness. I found comfort in the familiar discomfort of not-enoughness. Because believing I was flawed felt safer than risking the truth that I might already be lovable. If that were true, I'd have nothing left to hide behind. No excuses. No rehearsed suffering. I'd have to step fully into my life, and that kind of freedom? Terrifying.

Maybe you do this too.
You cradle your wounds and call them facts.
You hold others with compassion and hold yourself to impossible standards.

Ever caught yourself saying something like this?

"Listen, I don't think you understand. I can't just believe in myself, I've got a detailed file labeled 'Evidence I Suck,' complete with footnotes and cross-referenced case studies. I've spent years curating it. Decades. What kind of person would I be if I ignored all that hard work? And life? Oh, no, it's not just a phase, it's objectively terrible. Don't try to tell me otherwise. I have charts. Pie graphs. A color-coded trauma timeline. Don't rob me of my suffering, I've earned this melodrama. Besides, if I did believe something new was possible, what would I even do with myself? Start dreaming again? Risk disappointment? No thanks. I prefer my cozy little cave of fear. I've feng shui'd it. There are throw pillows and WiFi. Sure, growth is beautiful and expansive

and blah blah blah, but have you tried a solid spiral of self-sabotage followed by a nap? Absolutely delicious. So please, keep your positivity talk to yourself. I'm very busy convincing myself I'm not ready. It's basically my life's work."

Phew.

But here's the thing: pain that goes unchallenged becomes identity.
I had to unlearn the lie that worthiness was conditional.

So I began to rewrite the story.
Instead of *I'm not enough*, I said:
I am learning.
I am evolving.
I am important, not because of what I do, but because of who I am.

It wasn't easy. The old stories fought back.
But each time I chose truth over fear, I felt freer.

Self-worth isn't a finish line.
It's a choice you return to—again and again.
A reclaiming.

And when you embrace it, truly embrace it, the world doesn't have to change.
You do.
You stop asking if you belong.
You start walking like you do.
And that makes all the difference.

The more I honored who I truly was, the clearer the call became, and it began to lead me in an entirely new direction.

THE SHIFT

There came a point on my journey when the path felt less punishing, not because the terrain had changed, but because I had.

I wish I could say there was one defining experience I could carry like a talisman, something to hold onto when things got hard again. But it didn't happen all at once. It unfolded slowly, quietly, over the miles I walked.

For weeks, I had been moving through the densest parts of my shadow in the wilderness. Gradually, I began to make peace with them. I wasn't afraid of the darkness anymore. I could sit with it, breathe with it, even rest in it. What once felt like a threat now felt like a doorway. I no longer needed noise to distract me or people to fill the emptiness. I began to genuinely enjoy my own company. The quiet no longer felt scary—it felt vibrant, alive, even reverent.

One night, deep in the Badlands of South Dakota, I lay on a blanket spread over cracked earth. There were no city lights, no distractions, only wind whistling through rocks, the faint scent of dry sagebrush, and a stillness that wrapped around me like a worn blanket when the world finally lets you rest.

The sky above was blacker than black, so dark it felt infinite. Scattered across that velvet void were stars unlike any I had ever seen. Not faint twinkles from behind suburban haze, but radiant, raw, diamond-like sparks. Some sharp, some soft, all impossibly alive.

And then I saw it: the Milky Way stretching across the sky like a cosmic river, ancient and undisturbed. Stars scattered in every direction, some pulsing, others burning so brightly they seemed close enough to touch. A shooting star streaked across the horizon, so fast I almost doubted it had happened. Constellations emerged—Orion, Cassiopeia, the Big Dipper—like old friends guiding me from above. Even distant planets flickered with their own subtle glow, holding court among the stars.

My heart ached with the beauty and the vastness, tears welled before I even knew why. I lay there, tiny and awake, held by the earth beneath me and the stars above, staring up into the map of everything.

I wouldn't have seen it if I'd stayed in the light, in the places that felt comfortable, curated, and known. This kind of brilliance only reveals itself in the dark. And in that instant, I understood: Some things can only be seen when you're willing to leave the brightness behind. Some revelations only arrive when you're brave enough to lie down in the dark and look up.

Within that stillness, I heard something I hadn't heard in a long time: my own voice.
Not the inner storyteller.
Not the fearful child.
Not the demands of someone else's expectations.
But the pull of my own heart.

It began to reveal new things to me, a map forward. Not drawn in straight lines, but traced in wisdom, intuition, and lived experience. I had walked through fire. Sat beside grief. Spoken to my younger self. Reclaimed pieces I had exiled—and some I hadn't even known were there.

And now, as I rested in this clearing, something new emerged: a desire not just to survive the wilderness, but to integrate it. To weave what I had discovered back into the fabric of my life.

I no longer wanted to leave my journey behind.
I wanted to carry it with me.
Not the suffering, but the wisdom.
Not the pain, but the perspective.
Not the quiet, but the life it had gifted me.

What rose in me was clarity, a deep, grounded knowing that I could no longer return to who I had been. The wilderness had changed me. What I had unearthed along the trail wasn't just insight, it was direction. A reminder to honor what I know inside, and to lead with it.

I began to write down what surfaced, words, fragments, and sparks of insight. Not to record the past, but to illuminate the path ahead. The more I listened inward, the more I realized I wasn't just healing, I was reimagining. I wasn't just recovering, I was awakening.

And with that awakening came a fire of curiosity and possibility. I started to ask not only *what do I want to heal?*—but *how do I want to live?*

What would it mean to create a life not rooted in reaction, but in alignment? A life that felt expansive, embodied, and free.

The more I followed that question, the more I felt the stirrings of something I had never dared to name before: the longing for real freedom, not the version I had been sold, but the kind my spirit had always known.

Dear Fellow Journeyer,

There comes a moment on this path, one that is both terrifying and sacred, when you realize you can no longer build your life on the fragile foundation of seeking approval, proving your worth, or dimming your light to fit into places that were never meant to hold you.

It is the gateway between the life you were taught to accept and the life you were born to create.

You are standing at that edge now, and I know how tender it feels. I know the fear of shedding old identities, the discomfort of releasing familiar patterns, the uncertainty of stepping into the unknown without guarantees. But I also know this: a life built on self-worth will never betray you.

When you begin to rebuild, not from fear, not from lack, not from the desire to be chosen, but from the deep, unwavering knowing that you matter, everything begins to change.

The choices you make.
The relationships you welcome.
The boundaries you hold.
The way you speak to yourself in the quiet.

You no longer accept crumbs when you remember you deserve a feast. You no longer shrink to avoid rejection, because you've come to understand that true belonging starts within. You no longer trade your truth for temporary peace, because you've learned that discomfort is often the doorway to liberation.

And sometimes, before you can rise, you must go dark.
Not because you're lost, but because there are certain revelations, certain kinds of beauty, that only reveal themselves in the stillness of night. The dark teaches you to listen. To feel. To remember what you've forgotten in the chaos.

It is no detour—it is the path.

This road is not easy, but it is real.
There will be grief for the version of you who didn't yet know their dignity.
For the one who gave endlessly, waited too long, and worked so hard to be enough.

There will be times when the old ways call you back—familiar, safe, seductive in their
predictability.
But hear this:
You did not walk through fire to retreat into ashes.
You did not come this far to betray yourself now.

Keep walking.
Keep choosing.
Keep rising.
Not just once, but again and again and again.

This is your life.
Build it like you believe in yourself.
Because you are worthy of every radiant thing still ahead.

TRAIL WISDOM

FOLLOW YOUR HEART

Your heart is not reckless, it's wise in ways the world may never understand.
It doesn't speak in logic or timelines.
It speaks in pulses, in desires, in quiet inner knowings.

When you follow your heart,
you're not chasing a dream, you're honoring your worth.

Because to follow your heart is to believe
you are worthy of love, of joy, of fulfillment.
Worthy of the life that speaks to you when the world is still.

You don't have to earn that kind of life.
You only have to trust you deserve it.

And then take the next step—
not because it's easy,
but because you finally believe you're worth the journey.

PATH TO FREEDOM

Take a deep breath.

Feel the ground beneath you—solid, firm, and alive.
The roots below hold you.
The stones remember you.
The path rises to meet you, secure beneath each step.

You are walking toward freedom, not because it waits somewhere ahead, but because it lives within you, and each stride draws you closer to its center.

The wind doesn't resist you. It moves alongside you, urging you forward, lifting the last remnants of doubt you've outgrown. The burdens you once carried, other people's opinions, old traumas, fading identities, unravel like loose threads in the breeze.

You are lighter now. Stronger.

The trees thin around you, standing like witnesses to your emergence. Radiance spills across the open landscape, not hollow, but vibrant. Teeming with possibility, with space to breathe, stretch, and simply be.

As you step into that brightness, clarity settles inside you. Your heart beats steadier. Your body softens, no longer bracing, no longer hiding.

The air vibrates with a deep knowing: You are arriving.
Not because fear has vanished, but because you refuse to let it hold you back.
Not because you have every answer, but because you trust the path to keep unfolding.

And when you finally turn to look behind you, when your gaze traces the winding trail you've traveled, you don't see regret.

You don't see mistakes.
You see the journey—
the courage in every stride,
the grace in every fall,
the unraveling inside every breaking.

This is not the end.
It's the beginning of walking in your wholeness, rising in your truth, and standing in the life you were born to claim.

A WAY FORWARD

I knew I wanted a way forward. Something I could take back home, not just as a memory, but as a way of being. I didn't want to lose everything I had uncovered in those wild, transformative places the moment I stepped back into cell service, laundry piles, and inboxes filled with "just circling back."

I needed a way to carry the stillness I found into Monday mornings. To feel unburdened in the routines of life. To not get pulled back into the vortex of distractions and mindless motion. To feel spacious even while folding towels or unloading the dishwasher.

I wasn't looking for the kind of freedom that fits neatly into Facebook captions or life coach slogans. Not the "quit your job and move to Bali" kind of freedom (though, believe me, I've considered it). I longed for something deeper, the kind of freedom that cracked me open, peeled away the false layers, and asked, gently but insistently: *Who are you when no one's watching?*

Which led me to wonder—what is freedom, really?

For years, I thought it meant choice and expansion. The ability to live wherever I wanted, surround myself with people I loved, and live focused on the things that nurtured my spirit. I imagined it as having the resources to say yes to adventure, but also to rest. To slow mornings, long conversations, and uninhibited creativity.

But that wasn't the life I had been living. I stayed in a job that drained me. In relationships marked by pain more than support. I filled my days with endless doing—working, producing, managing—until there was barely any space left for joy. Somewhere along the way, I had mistaken survival for freedom, hustle for purpose, and sacrifice for love.

And yet, freedom didn't arrive in one grand instant. No fireworks. No chorus of angels. No neon sign. I found it in the Tetons, halfway up a trail I hadn't planned to hike, when the trees parted just long enough for the valley to pour its vastness into me. No epiphany. No revelation. Just silence, space and breath. It was my first true taste of inner freedom, not the achievement-driven version I had spent years chasing, but a shift in awareness that had been there all along.

I sensed it watching bison roam beneath the vast sky of Yellowstone, where the land made me feel both small and infinite. I experienced it in the Blue Ridge Mountains as the wind moved through golden grasses, unhurried, like it had all the time in the world. I touched it wading into the cool waters of Lake Michigan, sunlight glinting like scattered stars. Each glimpse brought me back to myself.

Freedom wasn't something to earn, prove, or chase. It was something I could inhabit—in my lungs, in my heart, in the simple act of being alive.

This was the beginning—the moment I realized the way forward wasn't out there waiting to be found. It was already inside me. That was the true opening: a return to myself, to a life that didn't just look good from the outside but felt honest at the core.

I began to unlearn the lies I had mistaken for truth: that productivity equaled worth, that love had to wound, that self-sacrifice was the price of belonging. True freedom doesn't require permission. It is presence.

But here's the thing: freedom, once glimpsed, must be chosen again and again. It's telling the truth, even when it's awkward. It's walking away from what harms you, no matter how familiar. It's choosing what feels right, whether or not others understand.

It's in the smallest things, the first sip of tea in the morning, a breeze through an open window, sunlight spilling across the floor. It's walking barefoot in the grass, kissing in the rain, laughing for no reason except that your spirit feels light again.

This is what I'm learning to choose.
And maybe, if you're here, it's calling to you too.

But learning to choose what matters isn't always graceful. It doesn't happen all at once. It begins with small reckonings, openings that ask you to stop pretending and start paying attention.

For me, it started long before I even had the words for it.

TRUTH THAT SETS YOU FREE

For much of my life, I believed that if I was agreeable, easy to love, and always put others' needs before my own, I would be safe. That if I was compliant and quiet, I could avoid conflict and escape rejection.

But silencing my voice never protected me, it only suffocated me. I told myself it was the price of being "good": sacrifice, compromise, and swallowing the words I wanted to speak. Yet the deeper truth within me was patient. It waited. And when it finally rose, it asked: *Will you keep pretending, or will you finally say what's true and real?*

Radical honesty is not just about what you say, it's how you live. It's refusing to forsake yourself in order to keep love. It's removing the mask, the smile, the over-functioning, the "No worries, I'm fine."

Before you can name what's real, you may camp out in denial. You justify. You over-explain. You dress red flags up as "opportunities for growth." But misalignment always catches up. It settles into the body, even when the mind refuses to name it.

Living honestly isn't about being loud or blunt. It's about integrity—choosing clarity over compliance, self-respect over self-sacrifice, and learning to live from the inside out.

When I finally listened to the inner voice of wisdom I had unearthed on the trail, I had to face the hardest truth of all: I had built a life that looked good on paper, but inside, I was slowly dying. Telling the truth, first to myself, then to others, was a radical shift. Because with truth comes choice. And choosing yourself requires raising your standards.

For too long, I called it selfish to want more. But raising your standards isn't self-centered, it's self-honoring. It's saying: *I am no longer available for what diminishes me.* With higher standards come boundaries. Not walls, but doors you choose to open and close. A boundary doesn't control others, it upholds you. It says: *This is what I will allow. This is what I will not.*

At first, setting boundaries feels clumsy. People who benefited from your silence may push back. They may call you self absorbed, difficult, or "not who you used to be." And they're right. You're not.

I lost people. I was judged. I grieved. But with every loss came liberation. Because when you say yes to your own self-respect, you may lose approval, but you gain something greater: self-trust. That's when relationships shift. You stop building them from a persona and start building them from authenticity. You stop diminishing yourself for peace and start living in integrity.

On the trail, there was no one else to tell me the way. No GPS to guarantee the "right" path. I was responsible for my own pace, my own choices, and my own steps. At first it felt terrifying. But over time it became empowering. Because when no one else directs your journey, you learn to listen to your own compass.

This is the freedom of inner authority: the clear voice that says, *I know what's right for me, even if no one else sees it yet.*

It doesn't mean you're never afraid. It means that when fear arises, you don't run from yourself. You turn inward. You listen. You follow. And when rooted in compassion, inner authority becomes a bridge between truth and love:
I can speak my truth and still be kind.
I can disappoint someone and still be worthy of love.
I can walk away and still be whole.

Because here's the truth: you cannot live fully while keeping parts of yourself hidden. You cannot honor your wisdom while living for validation.

Real love—whether from a partner, a friend, or yourself—will never require your silence. Those meant to walk with you will make space for your truth, even if it takes them time to understand. Some will leave. Some will stay. But above all, you must not leave yourself.

So I continue to speak. To listen. To trust. Because the world doesn't need more silence. It needs honesty, spoken with compassion, and grounded in love.

Telling the truth was the beginning. Living it required more. It wasn't enough to say what I knew. I had to become someone who stood by it. And that meant learning to build what I never had before: a trust I could finally lean on.

That's where devotion came in.

THE PATH OF DEVOTION

I had always appeared strong—driven, ambitious and resilient. I rebuilt what was broken, took bold leaps, and survived what could have undone me. But within that strength was a small, hairline fracture: the part of me that questioned whether I was truly capable of becoming the woman I longed to be. I had learned how to be strong for others, but I hadn't yet learned how to be strong for me.

That became another turning point: realizing that self-trust isn't something you're born with, it's something you build. Not through perfect plans or noble intentions, but through action. Every time I followed through on a promise to myself, I strengthened my integrity. Every time I turned away from what I knew to be true, I chipped away at my own foundation.

Self-trust doesn't vanish in a single moment. It slips away quietly, as self-doubt creeps into the spaces between intention and distraction. And as trust wavers, fear finds its opening.

The trail became my teacher. Mile after mile, with nothing to rely on but my breath, my instincts, and the steady cadence of my feet, I listened and learned. There was no one to validate me. No one to chart my course. No rescuer with a lantern or a pep talk. There was just me, and the next step.

Somewhere along the way, I understood: self-trust isn't a thought. It's a devotion. A vow you return to, especially when you want to turn back. Devotion is not a burst of motivation. It's an unrelenting commitment to what matters most. It steadies you when inspiration fades, when clarity disappears, and when no one is watching.

And devotion builds sovereignty.

Sovereignty is the rooted power of radical responsibility, the refusal to outsource your worth, your direction, or your healing. It means no longer handing the pen to another to write your story. No longer waiting for permission to take up space, to speak, or to create what you desire. It's standing in the center of your own life, trusting your inner compass, even when the world offers conflicting directions.

Yet even as I devoted myself to a new way of being, I still clung to control. I believed control made me safe. If I could plan far enough ahead, anticipate every possibility, manage every outcome, I could avoid disappointment. I mapped out my life like a blueprint: marriage by thirty, a beautiful home (preferably with a soaking tub and a front porch swing), children, a thriving career. When it all unraveled, I assumed I had failed.

What I didn't yet know was that control is a well-decorated illusion—a fortress of to-do lists, backup plans, and just-in-case scenarios, hollow at its core. It may shield you from risk, but it also numbs you to joy. What looks like control is often fear in disguise—fear of failure, of loss, of not being enough. And in time, control becomes a prison, built by your own hands, brick by careful brick.

It took everything falling apart for me to finally see it. And in that undoing, I let go. For the first time, I moved through life without a plan. I listened—to the land, to my body, to the beat of my own heart. I moved when I was ready. I rested when I needed. I stopped striving, and I began to allow.

In that surrender, I found a deeper calm.
I wasn't waiting for life anymore—I was in it.

This is what Grace taught me most. She didn't carry expectations, she simply was. If the sun was shining, she sprawled in it. If it rained, she shook it off. If she was tired, she napped—anywhere, anytime, and without apology.

Her way of being taught me more about surrender than any book or course ever could. Because surrender doesn't mean giving up. It means releasing what was never yours to control. It means choosing trust over fear, flow over force and willingness over resistance.

You surrender when you stop trying to change people who don't want to change. When you accept that timing isn't yours to dictate. When you loosen your grip on what should be and open up to what could be.

At first, surrender feels like falling—unmoored, uncertain.
But over time, it begins to feel like flight.

THE SACRED ART OF LETTING GO

Surrender also requires something deeper: faith.
Not just faith in the universe, but faith in yourself.
Faith that even without a plan, you'll find your way.
That even in the fog of uncertainty, you're being guided somewhere meaningful.

Faith isn't handed to you. It's cultivated in the very moments you want to turn back. It grows when you keep walking, not because you're confident, but because you sense there's something waiting on the other side.

On my journey, I often had to walk by faith alone. Not the kind you read about in books—the real kind. The kind you need when you haven't seen a trail marker in an hour and everything starts to look like the same tree. Sometimes the trail disappeared altogether. Other times it split into confusing forks with no signs, no logic, and certainly no ranger with answers. I had to rely on my instincts, my body, and Grace—who, unlike me, never questioned the path and always knew when it was time to stop and go for a swim.

Over time, I began to pay attention differently. I noticed signs not drawn on maps: the bend of the trees, the feel of the earth, goosebumps from a sunrise that felt like a holy secret. I listened for the stillness that whispered yes when I was on the right path. And I began to trust that some force, within and beyond, was walking with me.

Faith taught me to pause.
To breathe and listen.
Not for instructions, but for alignment.
Not to be told what to do, but to trust what felt right in my body.

That's the thing about surrender and faith: they aren't born in certainty. They're forged in the wild, in the moments when you stop forcing life into your timeline and start allowing it to unfold.

Faith isn't about walking alone. It's remembering you're co-creating with something greater. Your part is to show up, take the next step, listen inward—and believe that what you long for is already moving toward you.

When you lean in, breadcrumbs appear.
Doors open.
The right people arrive.
Not because you controlled it, but because you trusted it.

But here's the catch: you can't trust life if you're at war with yourself. That's where self-compassion comes in. Not as a soft platitude, but as a fierce kindness. The choice to stop punishing yourself for pain. To soften instead of harden when things don't go as planned. To rest, not because you earned it, but because you need it.

Self-compassion is the root of self-trust. The radical acceptance that you don't have to be more perfect or more healed before you belong to yourself. That nothing in you is broken. That your mistakes and your growth are part of your wholeness.

And that kind of acceptance is life-giving. Because when you stop rejecting yourself, you stop waiting for the world to tell you who you are. You stop pulling back. You stop hiding. You start showing up, with clarity and a heart wide open.

And that's when surrender begins to feel like freedom. You no longer need to know where the path leads. You just need to trust that you're meant to walk it. Not with perfection, but with devotion, faith, and love.

Devotion taught me to stay. To show up when things got hard. It also meant facing the past I carried—the shame, the regrets, the dormant stories in my cells. If I truly wanted freedom, I had to do more than walk toward what's next. I had to look back, with love, and carry forward only the wisdom.

EXTRACTING THE GOLD

I carried regret like a stone tucked deep in my backpack—invisible but persistent. No matter how far I walked or how much I grew, it lingered. In still moments it surfaced, muttering, *you should have known better.*

I replayed the choices I wished I could undo, the times I turned away from myself, the patterns I repeated, the people I hurt, the dreams I shelved. I stayed too long in what I had outgrown, convinced that if I had chosen differently, I'd be living a better life, or at least be a better version of myself.

But regret doesn't change the past. It just keeps you rehearsing the same scene, hoping the ending will change. Eventually I had to face the truth: no amount of shame or self-punishment could lead to fulfillment. The only way forward was release. Not forgetting or pretending, but choosing to stop beating myself up for what I didn't yet know. The work was to extract the lesson, integrate the wisdom, and—deep breath—begin again.

So I asked myself: *If I carried the wisdom instead of the shame, what would it be?*

That question opened a doorway, inviting me to look back at my choices with softer eyes, to see the lessons beneath the pain. I saw how I had stayed in relationships too long because I was still learning how to honor my worth, how the love I gave away so freely was the very love I withheld from myself. The relationship that broke me wasn't proof I was unlovable, it was a mirror of what I'd been settling for. And the version of me who made those choices wasn't powerless, she was surviving the best way she knew how.

This is the gold inside the pain. Every experience, no matter how messy, holds some kind of wisdom. And once embodied, wisdom changes how you live. It asks you to stop reenacting old stories. To break the cycles and choose again.

But you can't begin again until you tell the truth about the story you've been living. I had lived by one that told me I was stuck, my past defined me, and lasting change wasn't possible. It insisted love would always slip through my fingers, warned that trust was dangerous, and demanded I hustle endlessly to prove my worth.

And beneath that were even quieter beliefs:
That being loyal meant staying, even when it hurt.
That people would always leave.
That I was destined to be alone.

These beliefs became my navigation system, steering me off course. I longed to be someone's priority, even while unconsciously pushing people away. I tried to prove my worth by over-giving, over-functioning, over-explaining—like life was one long job interview I couldn't afford to fail.

But here's the thing: the stories you believe shape the way you live.
If you believe you're powerless, you act powerless.
If you believe you're not enough, you sabotage.
If you believe change isn't possible, you stay the same.

Rewriting your story is a soul retrieval. It's the conscious decision to stop defining yourself by pain or expired identities. To choose courage over repetition and aligned action over avoidance. To release control and learn how to trust, yourself, the process, and what's unfolding.

The backdrop of my life kept changing, but the story stayed the same—until I finally asked: *What am I still carrying that belongs to a former version of me?* And when I chose differently, the story began to rewrite itself.

In doing so, I didn't just change my life, I disrupted generations of inherited narratives. Stories passed down like fine china and emotional debt:
Survival mattered more than safety.
Anger replaced connection.
Self-sacrifice masqueraded as love.

But I chose something else:
Healing over inheritance.
Creation over repetition.
Freedom over fear.

Because healing doesn't just transform your life, it ripples outward. It touches every life you intersect. It heals backward and forward in time.

But naming the pattern isn't enough. You have to live the new story. Not with mastery, but with dedication. With every boundary you set, every truth you speak and every time you choose the present over the past.

Living the new story is a daily practice, unfolding moment by moment, choice by choice. And for me, those choices weren't just metaphorical, they were literal. Each step on the trail became a sentence in that new story. Not one written in fear, but in trust, clarity, love, and grace.

And with each stride, I felt it: lighter, freer, more open to life. I was no longer circling the same old pain. I was finally answering the call of my spirit, the one whispering all along: *This way. It's time to come home.*

Rewriting the story freed me from the past.
But there was one more release left to make.
Forgiveness.

UNSHACKLING THE HEART

On my journey, the two emotions that weighed heaviest in my backpack were anger and grief. I carried anger toward my parents, for the love that felt inconsistent, for the absence that shaped my childhood. I resented the fear, anger and chaos that filled our home. I was angry—at them, at life, at God—for failing me in the exact ways I most needed to be held. A part of me latched on to the belief that if I had truly been loved, things would have turned out differently.

Grief hit just as hard. I grieved what I had lost, what I never received, and what I knew would never come. I longed for a healing kind of love, something that might fill the emptiness left by unmet needs and unfulfilled dreams. I grieved the life I thought I would have, the plans that never came to be, the innocence stolen before I understood how much I would miss it.

For a long time, I didn't realize how tightly I was holding onto the victim story. It gave me something familiar to cling to, someone to blame, and a reason to make sense of the pain. But the longer I stayed in that story, the more it cost me. Because when you live as a victim, you unknowingly hand your power to the very people or circumstances that hurt you. Forgiveness asked something far more radical of me: to take my power back, not by pretending my emotions didn't exist, but by choosing not to let them define who I am.

But I had always struggled with forgiveness. In some ways, the pain felt like the only proof that what happened to me mattered. I wanted the people who hurt me to see the error of their ways, to own their behavior, and acknowledge the times they had disappointed me. I wanted to be right. I wanted to be seen. And I wanted an apology that might never come.

The truth is, at the time, I didn't understand what forgiveness really meant. I thought it was about excusing harmful behavior, minimizing the hurt, or making peace with people who had broken my trust. What I eventually learned is that forgiveness isn't about condoning the past. It's about reclaiming the future.

Forgiveness is the choice to release the burdens of what cannot be undone.
It does not mean excusing, forgetting, or inviting harm again.
It means deciding not to let the past dictate the rest of your life.

Healing wasn't about rewriting the past. It was about releasing the fantasy that it could have played out any other way. I spent years replaying moments in my mind, as if by analyzing them enough, I could change them, the relationship that didn't last, the betrayal that shattered my trust, the decision that led me somewhere I didn't want to be. I tortured myself with the thought: *It wasn't supposed to happen this way.*

But what if that thought was the very thing keeping me stuck?
What if that was the trap door beneath me all along?

That question followed me as I walked—mile after mile, trail after trail. And then, one midday in the Colorado mountains, something in me finally became willing to let go.

Blue Lake shimmered in full sun, clear and glassy, with glacial hues of teal and silver-blue that seemed almost unreal. The water was so still it mirrored the jagged granite peaks that circled the basin, their snow-streaked faces rising sharp and unyielding against the sky.

The alpine air was thin and bright, scented with high meadow grass and sunlit spruce. Snowmelt trickled down through the rocks. Along the lake's edge, bursts of wildflowers leaned into the breeze—tiny purple asters, yellow alpine sunflowers, and the occasional stalk of fireweed, bold against the pale earth.

A marmot darted between boulders, unbothered. Grace trotted ahead, her tail swaying with ease, pausing now and then to sniff the wind as if she sensed something just beyond reach.

Everything felt open and clear.
Unadorned and pure.

I knew this was where I needed to release what I had carried for too long.
I sat on a flat rock at the water's edge, pulled out my journal, and let the dam break.

I wrote a letter, not one I ever planned to send—a letter of forgiveness. I named every person I still held resentment toward—family, lovers, friends, people who had let me down, and people I had hurt in return. I wrote down every betrayal, every moment I was dismissed, manipulated, or diminished. I let the fury come.

And then I turned inward. I wrote to myself—
for the times I ignored my intuition.

For the ways I denied my own heart just to keep someone else close.
For the promises I made to myself but didn't keep.
For the ways I hurt others out of fear.
For the parts of me I had judged, silenced, or rejected.

When there was nothing left to write, I folded the pages in half and held them to my chest. Not as a farewell, but as a witnessing.
I see this.
I lived this.
And now, I'm ready to release it.

I undressed slowly, right there on the shore, the cool air brushing against my skin. I stepped into the lake, the cold pulling me back into my body. Every step a choice and every ripple a letting go.

Grace followed behind me, soaking in the coolness of the water and swimming in slow, gentle circles. She became a sacred witness to my ritual, a quiet presence holding space as I released what I no longer needed.

When the water reached my shoulders, I closed my eyes and sank beneath the surface.
Not to disappear.
But to cleanse.

I imagined the letter dissolving off of me—its ink, its sadness, its anger, its stories. Not erased, but transmuted. The lake didn't judge what I had written. It simply received it.

When I came up for air, I felt lighter.
Not entirely unburdened, I knew more would rise in time, but somehow cleaner.
As if I had finally stopped gripping the past like a weapon.
Like I no longer needed to prove how much it hurt.

By morning, the letter in my pack was water-stained and unreadable.
But the forgiveness was no longer on the page.
It was in me.

That moment didn't fix everything. But it gave me a new place to begin.

Life does not unfold according to our expectations. It unfolds exactly as it does. And while I may never fully understand why certain things happened the way they did, my power lies not in changing the past, but in deciding how I will move forward.

I had to release the illusion that things should have been different.
Life hadn't betrayed me, it had been carving me into someone new.

Every hardship, every heartbreak, every disappointment wasn't a detour from my story. It *was* the story and that's when I let go of the version of my life that only existed in my imagination.

Acceptance is not the same as sanctioning. It doesn't mean justifying someone else's actions or allowing the same cycles to repeat. It doesn't mean silencing the pain. It simply means no longer fighting reality. I stopped resisting the truth of what had already come to pass. I found the power to move forward, untethered from the chains of resentment.

But I also knew that forgiveness isn't a one-time act.
It's a process.

Forgiveness is something you have to choose again and again—when the hurt lingers, when no one takes responsibility, when the story replays without resolution, when the past creeps up on you, and when your body remembers before your mind does.

And in those moments, you remember the deeper truth:
forgiveness was never really about them.
It's always been about you.

That's when it hit even closer to home.
Because the hardest part wasn't forgiving them, it was forgiving myself.

I am the one I live with every single day. I can't escape my own reflection, my own memories, my own awareness of where I've fallen short. I've held myself to impossible standards, replayed the choices I regret, and punished myself for what I should have done differently.

I had to forgive myself—for not knowing what I couldn't have known until I had lived through it.

You may have resisted forgiving yourself because you believe that by holding onto shame, you're protecting yourself from making the same mistake again. But shame doesn't create growth. It creates paralysis.

True self-forgiveness isn't about forgetting or denying responsibility.
It's about recognizing that you are human.
That you are learning.
That you're allowed to make mistakes.

It's about holding yourself accountable with compassion instead of cruelty.
It's about understanding that you deserve the same grace you so freely offer others.

I used to believe that if I forgave, if I released blame, if I let go of the story that it should have been different, I would be left empty. Adrift. With nothing to hold onto.

But what I found was the opposite.
In letting go, I created space for something new.
In releasing blame, I reclaimed my power.
In laying down the weight, I finally learned how to rise.

Dear Fellow Journeyer,

There comes a moment—often quiet, often unexpected—when a deeper knowing rises to the surface. Not the polished narrative you've used to get by, but the raw, liberating kind, the kind that shatters old stories and says: This isn't who I am anymore.

That kind of truth is a beginning. Not the closing of your story, but the turning of the page.

It's the truth that sets you free.
Free from roles you never chose.
Free from dimming to be accepted.
Free from chasing love that costs your wholeness.

It calls you to step off the path of perfection and onto the path of devotion.

Because real transformation isn't found in having it all figured out, t's found in returning to yourself, again and again.
To your body.
To your breath.
To your inner wisdom.

Devotion isn't flashy. It's not about spiritual hustle. It's the silent vow to stay true to what's real, even when it's messy—choosing alignment over approval, speaking the truth even when you're terrified, honoring the fire in your belly and the softness in your chest.

Devotion is what roots you when everything in you wants to run. It's how you stay present with your spirit, even on the days you'd rather disappear.

But this path will also ask you to let go, of the version of you who had to prove, perform, or pretend, the dream that belonged to someone else, and the apology you're still waiting to receive.

Letting go is not defeat.
It's a sacred art. A holy act of self-respect.

Because once you release, something extraordinary happens:
you begin to extract the gold.

*The pain you've endured—the betrayals, the heartbreaks, the dark nights—
they hold wisdom, not because they were fair or justified, but because you survived
them. And in surviving, you were shaped, woven and forged.*

*You learned how to rise.
You learned what matters.
You found clarity in the ashes.*

*This is the alchemy of healing: turning pain into power, shame into insight, and grief
into grace.*

*But even then, there's one final threshold.
One final gate to your freedom.
Unshackling the heart.*

*This is the work of forgiveness.
Not forgetting. Not excusing.
But choosing to stop carrying what was never yours to hold.*

*To forgive is not to say "it didn't matter."
It's to say "I matter too much to let it keep hurting me."*

*It's the fierce decision to offer yourself the grace you've been waiting for.
To say: I release you, not for your sake, but for mine.*

And more than anything, it's the moment you stop betraying yourself.

*You may still feel the pain of what was lost, the love that never came, the innocence
that was taken, but you'll grieve with your heart open.
Not armored.
Not ashamed.*

And that changes everything.

*So wherever you are right now, whether you're just beginning to listen to the truth
inside you, standing in the fire of release, gathering gold from the rubble, or gently
unlocking your own heart—*

*Know this:
You are not behind.
You are rising.
And that rising is beautiful.*

TRAIL WISDOM

TRUST YOURSELF

The trail won't always be clear.
There will be days when the path disappears beneath your feet—
when the signs are weathered, the map is soaked,
and no one can tell you which way to go.

In those moments, trust yourself.
Trust the pull in your chest.
Trust the inner knowing that rises when you stop waiting for permission.
Trust the wisdom in your feet, your breath, your body's yes and your gut's no.

You weren't made to walk someone else's path.
You came here to walk your own.

You don't need to see the whole trail.
You just need the courage to take the next step.

EMBODYING THE LIGHT

Take a deep breath.

Imagine yourself standing at the edge of a mountain cliff. Behind you lies the winding path you've traveled—marked by steep climbs, deep valleys, and still riverbanks where you once paused to gather your strength. You've moved through darkness, through storms that tested your faith, through nights when you weren't sure the sun would ever rise.

And yet—you're here.
Grounded and changed.
With the wisdom of your journey imprinted on your soul.

Before you, in the distance, a glow begins to rise, an open meadow bathed in warm, golden light. The sun stretches across the horizon, casting long beams over the land, illuminating everything in its gentle, generous embrace.

This luminous glow is calling you forward.

As you step toward it, the light begins to meet you.
It washes over your skin, settles into your body, and fills the places where fear once lived. With each breath, its radiance softens the edges of all you've carried.

You've sat with your pain.
You've spoken your truth when silence would have been easier.
You've done the invisible work no one else could see.
And now, something within you is awakening.

Feel it in your chest—a steady ember pulsing.
With each inhale, it grows.
With each exhale, it spreads—through your fingertips, your words, and your being.
You are no longer only receiving the light.
You are the light.

Pause.
Claim it.
Let it ignite you.

Now, slowly, turn your gaze outward.

All around you, you see others, some stepping timidly into the unknown, some still wandering in their own wilderness. You recognize them. You've been where they are. You feel their longing for safety, their hunger for belonging, and their ache for something more.

And in this moment, something becomes clear:
Your journey was never just for you.
Every hardship, every act of courage, every realization was preparing you for this—
To carry the light forward.
To become a living reminder that healing is possible.

This is the holy work of the soul.
Not to escape the world, but to return to it transformed.
To awaken not only for yourself, but for the collective.
To heal forward and backward in time.
To walk not in search of light, but as its embodiment.

Let that truth settle into your heart, like the sun climbing to its peak.
This is not the end of the path. It's an evolution.

Now you walk not only for yourself, but for those who walk behind you.
You carry the torch. You are the guide.
A beacon. A reminder that transcendence is real.

Take another breath in. Let it anchor you.
Exhale slowly—offering that breath as a vow:
To walk with devotion.
To live with love.
To shine with the truth you've earned.
And to never again forget who you are.

THE GIFTS WE CANNOT SEE

I hesitated to claim my own gifts. From an early age, I felt a pull toward something greater, a deep knowing that spoke of purpose and expansion. But fear insisted it was out of reach. I didn't know how to turn that pull into something real, something lasting.

I tried, more than once. And still, I often found myself lost in the swirl of it all. I had always been creative, but so were plenty of others.

My mind scrambled with ideas, each one tugging me in a different direction like an over-caffeinated brainstorming session. I felt paralyzed by the possibilities, unsure of what was truly mine to share. I questioned whether my story, my voice, my way of seeing the world would ever land in anyone's heart. And underneath it all was the question I didn't dare speak out loud: *Did I really have what it takes to succeed?*

Still, I was determined. I poured myself into the things I knew how to do, hoping they'd be enough to keep me moving forward. Yet many of those paths led me back to the same place—pause, pivot, choose again.

Maybe you've felt this too. Maybe there's something inside you—a vision, a gift that's been with you since the beginning.
And yet, doubt rises.
Who am I to share this?
Who am I to take up space?

Here's what I've come to know:
None of us came here empty-handed.
We each carry something the world has never seen in quite the same way.

The question isn't *Do I have gifts?*
The question is: *Am I willing to bring them into the light?*

And this is where the golden shadow comes in.
Your shadow isn't only made of fear, shame, or pain.
It's not just the wounds or regrets you were taught to suppress or sanitize.
It also holds your brilliance, radiance and untapped potential.

Because shadow work isn't just about confronting what feels like too much or not enough. It's about reclaiming what you've been too afraid, too conditioned, or too humble to fully own.

The golden shadow holds your light—your genius, beauty and power.
It is the gift you secretly long to embody and the very thing you've been taught to dim, downplay, or push away.

Why do we do this?
Because claiming it feels risky.
It asks you to be seen in ways you're not sure you can survive.
To stand in fullness without apology.
To own your light without waiting for permission.

What if I'm wrong?
What if I succeed and still don't feel worthy?
What if I'm too much—or not enough?
What if I get hurt, rejected, or misunderstood?
What if people expect more than I can give?

So you tuck it away, right next to your wounds.
You bury your brilliance in the same shadowy corners where grief, rage, and tenderness have also been hidden and pretend it was never there at all.

But it is.
And it always has been.

There were long stretches when I did exactly that.
I questioned my value.
I squashed my light.

I compared myself until I was convinced I had nothing special to offer, that others could do it better, more polished, and with cooler websites and fonts.

But when you don't use what you've been given, something inside you begins to suffer, not because you're flawed, but because something essential is being denied.
That ache is a longing—for alignment, for expression.
When you ignore your gifts, you forfeit the joy of using them.
You grow restless and disconnected.
You wonder why you feel stuck, not realizing you're the one holding back the very parts of yourself that are meant to be shared.

So I got curious. I stopped searching outside myself and started paying attention to what had always been there, what felt effortless, what made me feel most like myself, even when no one else was watching.

I began to notice how people came to me, not just for answers, but for reflection. They came to feel seen and safe. To be reminded of who they truly were beneath all the noise and doubt. And in their reflections, I saw what I had struggled to recognize in myself: my courage, my creativity, and my capacity to hold space for transformation.

That's when I realized I had been carrying my gift all along.
I just hadn't claimed its full value.

Recognizing your gifts is one thing.
Believing in them is another.

I had to unlearn the lie that effort equals worth, that if it wasn't hard, it couldn't possibly be important. But the truth is, your most powerful offerings often come with ease.

The way you listen. The way you see.
The way you love, lead, create, or guide.

What feels obvious to you may be a revelation to someone else.
What flows effortlessly from you might be exactly what the world needs.

Your gifts don't have to be loud, flashy, or worthy of a TED Talk. They just need to be honored. Because what you offer, when anchored in love and truth, always matters.

But sometimes, even after you begin to see your gifts, you wait.
For the right moment.
For a certification.
For someone—anyone—to tell you you're ready.
You convince yourself you need more training, more time, and more confidence.

But what if people are already waiting for what only you can give?

NO MORE WAITING

Honoring your gifts is not just about seeing them, it's about embodying them. It's about the courage to claim your space. To be fully seen, even when fear would rather keep you silent, agreeable, and conveniently invisible.

I used to think stepping into my purpose meant proving something. That I had to earn the right to lead, to speak, to share—preferably with a five-step plan, a compelling backstory, and glowing testimonials.
But I was missing the bigger truth:
Our gifts aren't just about us.
They're about who we serve.

The words you speak may be the very words someone else needs to hear. The art you create, the presence you bring, the way you simply love—these might be the very things that keep someone going.

Maybe your gift is to guide, build, or disrupt systems that no longer serve. Maybe it's to hold sacred space, raise children with consciousness, or tend beauty in forgotten corners of the world. Or perhaps it's to listen deeply, ask brave questions, and remind others of their worth simply by being who you are.

You don't need permission to live as your fullest self, or a spotlight to make a difference. You just need the guts to show up, even if your hair's a mess and you're completely winging it.

A hand on someone's shoulder.
A truth spoken in love.
A refusal to give up on what matters.

These things ripple.
They heal.
They ignite.
They shift the world.

This is why you can't afford to keep hesitating. Because when you hold back, someone else is left without what only you can give. And when too many of us stay stagnant, the world doesn't evolve—it stalls. It begs for the voice you silence, the love you withhold, and the wisdom you keep hidden.

But when you step forward—imperfectly, courageously, unapologetically—something magical happens. You become a reflection of what's possible.
A permission slip.
A living, breathing catalyst for change.

For me, that invitation became clear.
I knew I was here to help others rise.
To move beyond limitation.
To reconnect with the parts of themselves they had buried or forgotten.

This path was never just about finding my deeper truth, it was about helping others reclaim theirs.

Because claiming your gifts isn't just a mindset shift.
It's a bold reclamation of your power.
A return to wholeness.
To what has always been true.

I no longer ask: *Who am I to share this?*
Now I ask: *Who am I not to?*

So I ask you the same.
No more waiting.
No more denying.
No more pretending you don't already carry something essential.

THE WHISPER IN THE WILDERNESS.

Toward the end of my journey, there was a morning I'll never forget—a moment so still, so reverent, I knew my life would never be the same.

The air was crisp, edged with that unmistakable scent of earth cooling overnight, a mingling of pine, soil, and river stone. It carried the last tender trace of summer, that faint sweetness lingering just before fall fully settled in. I could feel the shift in season not only around me, but inside me too, like something quietly turning.

A deep stillness lay over the land, the kind that makes you whisper even when no one's there. My breath rose in small clouds, visible in the dawn air. I pulled my sweatshirt tighter and tucked my hands into the sleeves, letting the chill seep into my limbs like a slow current, bracing, but alive.

In front of me, the Grand Tetons stood immovable, jagged silhouettes cutting into the fading dark like ancient stone guardians. They rose with an authority that didn't demand attention, it simply received it. Their peaks were still cloaked in the night's shadow, wrapped in deep blues and purples that would soon give way to fire.

The world felt suspended, as if holding its breath for the arrival of the sun. Even the birds hadn't begun their morning songs. There was no wind, only the faintest rustle in the trees behind me, like the earth itself was stretching awake. My senses sharpened; everything felt amplified.

I sat on a stone wall, its cool surface grounding me. Moss clung to the cracks, damp from the night air. My fingers traced the edge, pulling me into the present as I breathed in the faint scent of distant woodsmoke.

The sky began its slow transformation, soft ribbons of lavender and primrose unfurling across the horizon. Above the peaks, stars blinked out one by one, yielding to the rising light.

Beside me, Grace sat unmoving, her caramel fur catching the first gold like an offering. She was regal in her stillness—ears slightly lifted, eyes soft yet watchful, her breath steady beneath muscle and fur. She didn't move. She just watched—calm, alert, present—as if she had always known this moment would come.

A hawk soared overhead, carving the sky with effortless grace. The ridgeline loomed unyielding and timeless. And the valley, wide and open before me, held a beauty unlike anything I had ever known.

For the first time in my life, I wasn't afraid of being alone. The solitude didn't feel like isolation; it felt like communion. I wasn't just sitting in the wilderness—*I was the wilderness.* The hawk, the wind, the rising sun. I felt the presence of something vast and infinite, both within and beyond me. I imagined all who had come before—wanderers, seekers, those who had walked into the wild searching for themselves.

And then, in that first light of morning, it came.
A voice, not loud, but certain.
Not outside me, but within.

Go teach what you have come to learn.

It wasn't a thought or suggestion, it was deeper. A call that rose from my bones, so clear it couldn't be ignored.

I didn't know what it would look like—no map, no plan. Just a truth rooting itself in me like a seed, waiting to be tended.

I breathed it in, letting it settle. The mountains, the sky, the hawk, they weren't second-guessing their existence. They simply were. And if I was going to keep walking, I couldn't keep questioning mine either.

It was time.
To share my stories.
My shadows.
My truth.
To speak of the lessons I had gathered along the thousand-mile path.
To step forward—not just as a seeker, but as a guide.

The sun spilled gold across the land, casting everything in a breathtaking glow. I closed my eyes, lifted my face to the warmth, and let the tears fall. Then I took a long inhale and claimed my path.

And so I listened—not with my ears, but with something deeper: my heart, my body, my soul. The whisper I heard in the wilderness didn't hand me a step by step guide or a manual. It offered something far more useful: alignment.

It wasn't enough to hear the call. I had to respond.
To carry it down from the mountain into my everyday life.
To let it inform my choices, refine my focus, and anchor my devotion.

What I heard in that silence wasn't just guidance, it was a mirror. A reflection of the woman I was becoming, and the life that had been waiting for me to rise and meet it.

It wasn't some distant dream to chase.
It was something to embody.

That's when I began to understand the true nature of creation, not as something summoned from thin air, but as something unlocked from within.

Manifestation isn't magic—it's alchemy.
Not wishing, but transforming.
And that transformation doesn't happen out there.
It happens *in here*.

THE ALCHEMY OF CREATION

Before I started my journey, I misunderstood what manifestation truly was. I thought it meant making a vision board, speaking affirmations, and imagining the life I wanted until it arrived like a package on my doorstep—delivered by the universe because I had finally said the right words or thought the right thoughts.

I believed that if I could just align my energy, hold a positive mindset, and live in the vibration of gratitude, everything I wanted would flow to me with ease. And when it didn't, when life cracked me open, when things fell apart, when the vision didn't arrive on cue, I wondered if something was wrong with me. Maybe I wasn't clear enough. Maybe I was blocked. *Maybe I was the problem.*

The truth is, life doesn't bend to carefully curated desires. It asks more of you.

What I learned was that manifestation isn't about pretending. It isn't bypassing grief or skipping the hard parts. And it's certainly not about controlling outcomes with perfect thoughts or spiritual acrobatics. It's not waiting for something outside of you to change, it's becoming the version of yourself who can hold what you're calling in. Alignment isn't just thought; it's feeling, embodiment, and the way you move through the world.

Still, many of us stay stuck. We tell ourselves we don't really know what we want. But often, we do, we're just afraid of what choosing it might require. Afraid of getting it wrong. Afraid of failing. Afraid of what others will think if we step outside the mold. Afraid of the responsibility that comes with committing. So we remain in the gray space of confusion, convincing ourselves we need more time, more clarity, and more signs. But clarity rarely arrives fully formed. It unfolds through action.

When you stay lost in indecision, you send mixed signals to life. You inch forward, then retreat. You ask for one thing, but settle for another. Clarity is a compass, it cuts through the noise of doubt and distraction. And paradoxically, it often comes after the leap, not before.

We want certainty before we act. But in reality, action creates certainty. You don't figure out the path by standing still. You figure it out by walking it.

So ask yourself:

What do I truly want?

Not what you think you should want. Not what others expect. But what your soul hungers for. Be brave enough to name it. Let it rise and breathe.

And then move toward it, even if you're unsure, even if you're scared, even if the path isn't fully visible yet. Because wanting isn't enough. Manifestation requires embodiment. It asks you to become the version of yourself who can receive and sustain what you desire.

You don't attract what you want.

You attract who you are.

You can long for love, success, abundance, healing. But if your identity is still rooted in scarcity or unworthiness, you'll continue to recreate those patterns. Life responds not to your wish, but to your frequency.

If you want something new, you must become someone new—not by pretending, but by shedding what you've outgrown and returning to your essence.

When I started this quest, I didn't just wish for courage, I cultivated it, step by uncertain step. I didn't just dream of transformation, I lived it. In the silence. In the struggle. In the unraveling.

Manifestation isn't about high-vibe thinking or spiritual optics.

You can't speak abundance and act from fear.

You can't dream of love while bracing for loss.

You can't wish for change while resisting discomfort.

Everything must align.

Your mind must believe it's possible.

Your heart must feel the truth of it.

Your nervous system must feel safe enough to receive it.

Your body must move in its direction.

I learned this in the wilderness. When the trail felt endless and my legs trembled with fatigue, I kept my eyes on the next step—not the whole journey, just the one in front of me. That's the presence manifestation requires, not fixation on the outcome, but commitment to the process.

Because what you focus on grows.

Focus on what's missing, and you amplify lack.
Focus on what's possible, and you create possibility.

And none of it works without belief. If you don't believe in what you're calling in, you won't receive it, not because it isn't meant for you, but because you won't let it land. I had to believe in myself long before the world reflected it. I had to walk as the woman I was becoming, long before anyone else could see her.

Belief is not blind optimism. It's a decision.
A dedication to the unseen.
The courage to keep going while doubt still lingers.

The universe meets you at the level of your belief—
Not what you wish for, but what you claim.

But even belief isn't the final piece.
Manifestation isn't only about creating, it's about allowing.

You may be more comfortable in the struggle than in the receiving.
Good at the chase, but terrified of the arrival.
Praying for miracles, but expecting disappointment.

I had to learn how to soften. How to let love in.
To stop fighting for everything.
To realize some things were simply meant for me.
To stop pushing and start opening.
To stop proving and start receiving.

And above all, I had to practice gratitude.

On the trail, I came to cherish the simplest things, the warmth of the sun on my shoulders, the sound of running water, the strength in my body carrying me forward. Gratitude expanded everything. The more I noticed, the more there was to notice. The more I appreciated, the more aligned I became.

Gratitude is the vibration of already having.
Already being.
Already trusting that what you desire is on its way.

Gratitude says to the universe:
I see what you've given me and I'm ready for more.

So even now, before the dream is fully here, can you be grateful for the steps? For the lessons? This is the work. And when you show up for it—fully, truthfully, bravely—life will meet you where you stand.

Because in manifestation, just as in this journey, the most powerful moments aren't the ones where you reach a goal or cross a finish line. They are the moments when you realize that what you were searching for was already within you, waiting to be uncovered.

It was never about finding the right path—
It was about remembering I was the path all along.

I just had to trust what I'd been given, and allow myself to be seen, completely, without hesitation.

COMING HOME TO MYSELF

What this journey through the wilderness—both outer and inner—taught me most was that the path was never about becoming someone different. It was about shedding everything I thought I had to be in order to be loved, accepted, or safe. I set out looking for answers, longing for peace, desperate to release fear, hoping that somewhere along the trail I'd stumble upon the version of me I'd lost.

But what I found instead was something far more true:
She had never left.
She'd been there all along, waiting beneath the noise.
Buried under years of fear, conditioning, masks, and people-pleasing so refined it could've earned me a degree in emotional contortion.

This wasn't just a 1,000-mile walk.
It was a sacred return.
A descent into the unknown, and a rising into remembrance.

The wild unlayered me, piece by piece.
It revealed truths I didn't want to face.
It brought me to my knees and lifted me to my feet—again and again.
And in doing so, it taught me how to listen, feel and stay with the discomfort, not to fix it, escape it, or run from it, but to meet it with presence. To breathe through it.

I learned that freedom isn't found in the absence of struggle, but in the willingness to meet yourself inside it. That power isn't something you chase "out there"—it's something you reclaim when you stop betraying yourself. And that love—real, soul-deep love—doesn't begin with someone else. It begins within.

And now, I live from a different place. Not from managing, controlling, or contorting, though those habits still try to sneak in now and then. But from self-trust, alignment and integrity.

I am not who I was when I began.
But I am more me than I've ever been.

The moment you stop hiding, you begin to rise, not only for yourself, but for each other. For the collective. Shining your light, sharing your gifts, and allowing the truest parts of you to take their rightful place in the world.

The time is now.
The shadow calls.
And life is waiting for you to respond.

THE COLLECTIVE SHADOW

You are living in a time of reckoning, a time when the fractures in the world, long denied and carelessly patched over, are now split wide open. The cracks in the systems, in the stories, and in your very sense of what it means to be human are no longer hidden. They are staring you in the face.

The darkness that once lingered quietly in the corners has surged forward. It is loud now. Unignorable. It demands to be seen, named, and met.

You are witnessing the collective shadow in its rawest form, fear parading as righteousness, division disguised as protection, disconnection disguised as strength. Greed and power have become the engine of progress, and the wounds of generations are surfacing, not quietly, but in earthquakes, wildfires, and wars. In the silent breakdown behind closed doors.

We are unraveling, not because the world is ending, but because what is false can no longer hold. The old paradigms are crumbling. The stories that kept you small, compliant, divided, they're coming undone, thread by thread. The masks are slipping. The illusions you once clung to for comfort are dissolving in the heat of truth.

The world is not dying, it is awakening.
And as with any awakening, the dark must rise before the light can fully return.

This is not a time to look away.
This is not a time to stay silent.
This is the moment to lead.

Darkness does not disappear on its own.
It must be faced, named and transformed.

This is why your voice matters.
This is why your truth matters.
This is why your light is not a luxury, it is a necessity.

For centuries, the world has taught you separation, from each other, from the earth, and from your own body and wisdom.

Pain became power. Fear became policy. Suffering became currency.
You've been taught to numb with distraction, to silence your intuition with noise, and to mistake consumption for connection.

But the shadow is rising.

It shows up in war and violence, in systems built to exploit and divide.
It shows up in the erosion of empathy, in algorithms that profit from outrage, in the exhaustion of those told they must keep producing just to earn rest.
It shows up in the disconnection—the scrolling, stuffing down, and pretending.
It shows up in the lie that busyness will shield you from what's breaking inside.
It shows up in the fear that tells you to turn against each other and build walls instead of bridges. It shows up in the loneliness of a world that no longer knows how to sit in silence, to listen without reacting, or to see beyond the screens and the stories you've been sold.

But let this be known:
The shadow does not rise to destroy you.
It rises to ignite you.

It is a summons.
A gateway.
A divine disruption.

It is not here to pull you under.
It is here to call you back—back to truth, to each other, to yourself.

Because the only way through this collective darkness is not to run from it, but to walk straight into it—with open eyes, a strong heart, and the willingness to heal what lives within you.

This moment is not a mistake.
It's a beckoning.
To remember.
To rise.
To reclaim the light you were never meant to forget.

The world is waiting, not for you to have it all figured out, not for you to be fearless or flawless, but simply for you to show up.

A CALL TO RISE

Now is not the time to hold back.
Not a time to retreat, shrink, or wait for someone else to lead.

The world does not need more quiet compliance, more people playing small while fear takes up the loudest space in the room. What it is calling for are truth-tellers, healers, and visionaries. It needs creators, disruptors, and rebuilders of broken models and tired norms.

Your voice matters.
Your perspective matters.
You influence more than you realize.

Each time you speak truth, you send ripples through the collective.
Each time you show up authentically, you give others permission to do the same.
Each time you refuse to bow to fear, you shift the energy of the earth itself.

You don't need a massive platform to make an impact.
You don't need to be perfect to be powerful.
You just need to be who you are, wholly, freely, unapologetically.

In a world that profits from fear, living in love is a revolution.
In a world built on disconnection, choosing presence is a radical act.
In a world that silences truth, speaking from your soul is an uprising.

Your gifts—whether they are words, art, healing, teaching, leading,
or simply the way you walk through the world—are not nothing.

They are light. And light is the only thing that can dissolve the dark.
So if you've been waiting for permission, this is it.
If you've been waiting for the world to be ready, it won't be.
And if you think you must feel fully prepared, you never will. Do it anyway.

The planet doesn't need more spectators. It longs for courageous souls willing to rise, to speak, to embody the truth of who they are.

This is why you are here.
This is the moment you were made for.

Dear Fellow Journeyer,

I am writing to you from the depths of my heart to speak a truth you may already be starting to remember: the world needs you.

Right now, more than ever, the offerings you carry, those powerful, singular pieces of your being, are essential to the healing of this planet. You were never meant to hold them back or wait for the "right moment" to emerge.

It takes courage to walk through the wilderness. To turn toward your fear. To shed the stories that no longer fit.

The collective shadow—the fear, division, and disconnection all around you—is rising. It is asking to be seen and healed. But it is also a mirror, reflecting the places within you where you may have abandoned yourself in the name of approval or safety.

You cannot transform what you are unwilling to face. And you cannot change the world without first returning to wholeness within yourself.

This is where your radiance comes in.
The shadow cannot endure where presence shines.
Your essence—your voice, your truth, your authenticity—is that radiance.

This season of reckoning is also a season of remembering.
A call to embody who you truly are, and to honor the medicine you carry.

When you do, you become the catalyst.
The one who shifts the story.

You don't need to be perfect. You just need to arrive as yourself.

Each time you choose courage over fear, each time you refuse to shrink, you shine.
And that glow ripples outward, inviting others to do the same.

The moment is now, dear journeyer. The world is changing. Don't retreat in the face of uncertainty, rise in the name of truth.

Step on—imperfectly, courageously, and wholeheartedly.
And as you do, remember: the healing you long for begins within.

One brave, authentic step at a time.

TRAIL WISDOM

INSPIRE CHANGE

The trail doesn't change the landscape, it changes the traveler.
And yet, as you walk it, step by step, mile by mile, you become the change.
Not by preaching, but by living.
Not by shouting, but by showing.

Your courage to keep going, to rise after falling, to speak truth in a world that rewards silence, that's what inspires others to begin their own path.

You don't need to have it all figured out, just the courage to walk in alignment with what matters most.

Let your life be the message.
Let the way you love, lead, listen, and rise become the spark that lights the path for someone else.

EPILOGUE

THE RETURN

When my journey ended, I knew, even before I stepped back into the life I had left behind, that I could never return to it. It wasn't just the miles I had walked. It was everything I had shed along the way. I had followed the path until it became me, until there was no separation between the ground beneath my feet and the undeniable truths rising up from within.

I hadn't only crossed landscapes; I had laid down personas, released stories, and mourned identities I once grasped like armor. What remained was honest and real—and it no longer matched the place I once called home.

Within a year, I packed up my office, closed my therapy practice, and walked away from the world I had so carefully built. A world that had once given me purpose but, over time, became a cage—heavy with expectation, drained by burnout, and laced with disconnection. I hadn't failed it. I had simply outgrown it. Or maybe, for the first time, I had finally grown into myself.

The wilderness had shown me more than I imagined, stripping away illusions layer by layer. I had stretched beyond my edges, broken open in ways that changed me, and felt so deeply that I could never return to the smallness of what had been.

Even before I left, I sensed I was meant to create something different. I didn't know exactly what it would be, but when I returned, it was clear: it would be anchored in truth, alignment, rest, freedom, beauty, and a deep devotion to living a life that reflects the woman I had become. I wanted to take what the wilderness taught me and offer it back to others.

I met with my close friend George, a creative visionary who, like me, felt drawn to build something meaningful, something that could guide others through their own inner transformation. We sat in deep conversation, sharing stories, dreams, and the life-changing experiences I had on the trail. From those conversations, a vision began to ignite.

For the next year, we met weekly, pouring ourselves into the bones and breath of what would become known as *The Wilderness Walk*—a sacred passage into the shadows to dismantle the barriers, limitations, and inherited lies that keep us from becoming who we were created to be. What emerged was not just a program, but a raw, reverent initiation—an experience of change that invited others to awaken, rise, and embody the life they were meant to live; to honor their voice, power, and wisdom; and to return to themselves with permission to heal, release, and reclaim their brilliance.

We knew the work wouldn't be easy. True transformation never is. But we also knew this: the wilderness carries medicine. In descent, we uncover our strength. Through discomfort, we remember what matters most. And in the dark, we are led back to the light.

We wanted to offer others what my pilgrimage had sparked in me: the courage to say yes to their own evolution. Not everyone would walk a thousand miles, but everyone carries a wilderness within. And we knew the metaphor could live on as a mirror of the inner terrain we are each called to navigate: fear, doubt, love, joy, and the radiant aliveness waiting on the other side.

The Wilderness Walk was born as a rite of passage for the modern soul.
An initiatory passage inward.
A sacred reclamation.

THE CALL OF THE MOUNTAINS

It happened somewhere out west, between the raw, jagged beauty of the Grand Tetons and the expansive embrace of the Rockies. I remember the moment clearly, standing in the cool morning air, the mountains before me, majestic and timeless, touched by the first light of dawn. They weren't just mountains. They were sentinels—steadfast, silent, and impossibly old. They didn't speak in words, but in a language I felt at my core. An unseen energy moved through the wind, the rivers carving the valleys, and the silence that felt more powerful than noise. In their presence, I felt altered. A knowing. Not of thought or plan, but of soul—a recognition that defied explanation.

I longed for a home that would bring me back to myself. A sanctuary where quiet was honored, where the land offered wisdom if you were still enough to hear it. That morning, I knew, I didn't just want to visit the wild. I wanted to belong to it.

Colorado called to me because it offered everything I had been yearning for—clean, invigorating air that made me feel alive again, a way of living that nourished both body and spirit, and a slower, more intentional rhythm. I didn't know exactly where I'd land, but I trusted the right place would reveal itself. Somewhere I could put down roots, build community, and live more in communion with nature.

It would also be a haven for Grace. She was six when we moved, already going gray around the muzzle, but still so full of life. She loved being untamed, nose to the wind, paws in the dirt. Wherever I settled, it had to be a home for her too, a place where she could spend her years beneath open sky, wandering forest trails, unbound, resting on her own terms. She had walked so much of the path beside me. She deserved that kind of peace as much as I did.

A HARD GOODBYE

After arriving in Colorado, I lived in a few different homes over the years, always circling the mountains, always drawn to the stillness of the pines and the expanse of open sky.

I led transformational wilderness walks, holding space for others as they unearthed what had long been buried—grief, truth, desire, rage—and in time, hundreds found their way to the trail of their own reclamation. I guided journeys across California, Alaska, Costa Rica, Greece, and beyond—each landscape offering its own magic, each step a return to what had been forgotten.

And through it all, Grace was there. She walked beside me on every trail and curled at my feet as I sketched new dreams onto paper. She was my muse, the silent witness to my unfolding, the one who watched me rebuild a life from the ashes of another. She didn't need to speak to teach me. Her companionship was enough.

Over time, I watched her soften into her elder years. It happened slowly, then all at once. Her steps grew more careful. Her once-eager runs became deliberate strolls. The body that had bounded up rocky inclines now hesitated at the smallest hills. But she never stopped following me, not completely. She stayed close, always close, as if she knew our story was still being written.

She slept more, often settling into sunlit patches on the floor or her favorite corner of the couch. Sometimes I'd catch her watching me while I worked, her gaze calm and gentle, as if she saw a version of me I hadn't yet grown into, something she had always known was coming. She'd tilt her head, rest her chin on her paws, and release a sigh that seemed to carry lifetimes.

The day before Thanksgiving, I found a lump on her neck. Firm to the touch, the size of a golf ball—sudden and strange, as if it had appeared overnight. At first, I told myself it was probably a cyst, nothing serious, something benign that would fade on its own. But something in me resisted that reassurance. Deep down, I felt uneasy.

Still, I tried to stay composed as I drove her to the vet. The sky was gray, a muted November light that made the world feel heavier. Grace rode in the passenger seat, her head resting on the console, eyes soft but tired. She always seemed to know when we were headed somewhere she didn't want to be.

The waiting room was quiet. The smell of antiseptic clung to the air, sharp and sterile, while fluorescent lights hummed faintly overhead. Grace lay at my feet, her body trembling against my shoe. I could feel her warmth, her trust, the uneven rhythm of her breath. My fingers traced behind her ears again and again, trying to ground myself in the familiar texture of her fur.

When they called us back, the exam room felt colder than usual, the kind of chill that seeps beneath your skin. The stainless steel table gleamed under bright lights, clinical and unwelcoming. She hated being lifted onto it, so instead I sat on the floor with her pressed against me, solid and warm, as the vet knelt beside us.

She palpated the lump gently, her face composed but serious, quiet in that way that needed no words. The air in the room shifted, heavy with unspoken knowing. Something passed between us in the silence, and in that instant, I knew.

"We should biopsy it," she said. "It's likely a tumor."

I nodded, feeling numb. I don't remember what I said, only the way the room seemed to shrink around me, her voice fading beneath the thrum of my heartbeat. The walls closed in. My chest tightened. I couldn't catch my breath.

We ran the tests, and then I waited, like someone bracing for a verdict they already feared. When the call came, the biopsy confirmed it was malignant.

In a moment, everything changed. The world seemed to stop. I cried in a way that felt endless, primal—a cellular kind of grief, raw and consuming, known only to those who have loved that deeply.

I couldn't bear it.
But I had to.

We saw an oncologist and began treatment. I asked every question, researched every protocol, clung to every thread of hope I could find. But the cancer moved quickly—too quickly. I felt her slipping away, little by little. At night she still curled against me, but something was changing. Her energy was softer now, distant, like she was already beginning to let go.

Desperate for guidance, I brought Grace to an animal intuitive, a woman a friend had told me about. She lived outside of town in a small home beneath a stand of aspen trees. The air around her property was still, broken only by the honking of distant geese.

She opened the door barefoot, silver-streaked hair falling loosely around her shoulders, her eyes kind and deep. Her home smelled faintly of cedar and sage, warmed by firelight and filled with woven blankets, feathers, stones, and shelves of well-worn books.

She greeted Grace not as a pet, but as an elder. Kneeling slowly, she laid her hands on Grace's chest, then her neck, fingers resting just beneath the lump. She didn't speak—just listened, palms steady, and presence wide open.

The room held a holy stillness. Then, without looking at me, she said, "She's ready."

I nearly gasped.

"She's not in pain," the woman continued, "but she's tired. Her body is heavy. Her soul is wise. And she's holding on—for you."

Tears spilled before I could stop them.

"She's worried about how you'll handle her leaving. That's the only thing tethering her here."

I nodded, unable to speak. Grace lay beside me, calm and composed, as if she understood everything—more than I ever could—and needed nothing from me but closeness. Her head rested on my feet, ears relaxed, and her small frame tucked gently against me. Every so often, her tail gave a faint thump, a reminder: she was still here.

"She wants you to savor this time," the woman said softly. "Not in fear of losing her, but in gratitude for the love you've shared."

And so I did.

Over New Year's, I packed the car with her favorite blanket, some candles, her well-worn toys, and the memories we had made from peaceful weekends like this—ones I wasn't ready to say goodbye to. I drove us into the mountains, where a small cabin sat nestled beneath towering pines, dusted with fresh snow and wrapped in the stillness of winter. Just the two of us. No cell service. No outside noise. Just the crackle of the woodstove, the soft light of candles flickering against pine-paneled walls, and the steady cadence of her breathing beside me.

It was our final adventure.

We walked when we could, slowly along the snow-packed path behind the cabin. The world was quiet, except for the creak of branches and the distant call of a raven echoing through the trees. I made soup and sat on the couch wrapped in a blanket, her head in my lap as we watched the wind move through the trees outside the window. Time stretched long and tender.

I spoke to her often, not with words that needed answers, but in the language we had always shared, a wordless understanding, a love that asked for nothing but presence.

When we came home, the days that followed were gentle, fleeting. I could feel time slipping through my hands.

And then, in the early evening of January 11th, the life I knew ended.

Grace had been subdued that morning, less herself. She wouldn't eat, and when I looked into her eyes—once clear, familiar, and full of life—they seemed far away, as though she was already walking somewhere I couldn't follow.

And then, without warning, her body seized. She stiffened, legs twitching uncontrollably, breath breaking in sharp bursts. I dropped to the floor, cradling her head in my lap, whispering through tears that she was safe, that I was here, even as panic rose thick in my throat.

The vet confirmed what I already feared: the cancer had reached her brain.

I had promised her she would never suffer. That she would never die in a sterile exam room, beneath fluorescent lights, on a cold steel table she had always hated. She deserved more than that. She deserved peace. She deserved home.

Snow had been falling since dawn, heavy and relentless. I called every vet I could, desperate for someone to come to the house. Each call ended the same: no availability, roads impassable, I'm so sorry. Time was slipping fast.

And then, by what I can only call grace, the phone rang. A Denver clinic had just had a surgery cancel. One of their vets was willing to make the drive.

When he arrived, it felt like an angel had stepped through the door. He slipped off his jacket, snow still clinging to the sleeves. His frame was strong but unassuming, shaped by time outdoors. His smile carried a gentleness that soothed me. I noticed several tattoos on his arms, one a small paw print—a tribute, he later told me, to his own dog.

He didn't rush. He didn't speak in clinical terms. He knelt beside Grace with reverence, hand resting lightly on her side, voice soft, as if he knew he was in the company of something irreplaceable.

"You've done your job," he whispered. "You can rest now."

We lit candles, flames flickering in the dim light. I played *Shores of Avalon* by Tina Malia, a song I had always known would guide her home. The room transformed into something more than a living room, it became a sanctuary, a temple, a portal between worlds.

The vet gave her something for the pain. I lay down beside her, cradling her body in my arms, my face buried in the familiar fur behind her ears. I whispered every thank you I could: for walking with me, for loving me, for never leaving my side. I told her she was my teacher. My best friend. My wild-hearted girl.

And then, the final injection.

Her breath slowed. Her body softened. One last exhale.
And just like that... she was gone.
It was the hardest goodbye I've ever known.
Grace left this world as she lived in it—held, honored, and deeply loved.

THE ECHO OF HER ABSENCE

In the months that followed Grace's passing, the silence was the hardest part. Sometimes, I still heard her, phantom sounds rising in the quiet of the house. The soft thump of her paws bounding up the stairs. The gentle sigh as she settled into her favorite corner of the couch. The click of her nails on the hardwood floor. And always, the faint clink of her collar as she moved through the rooms. Every now and then, I would turn, expecting to see her there. But she wasn't.

In her absence, a hollowness opened, an emptiness I hadn't felt in years. Grief didn't come in waves. It settled like fog—slow, heavy, impossible to shake. It blurred the edges of everything. I kept moving through the days, doing what needed to be done, but nothing felt entirely real. She had always been there—my constant, my anchor, my home.

One day, longing for something—anything—I reached out to an animal medium. Not from superstition, but from hope, rooted in the deep knowing that Grace had always been more than a dog to me. I wasn't looking for answers so much as connection. I just needed to know she was still near, that the bond we shared hadn't vanished with her final breath.

We spoke over the phone. Her voice was gentle and warm, like someone who had spent a lifetime holding grief with tenderness. She asked only for my name and Grace's. Then she invited me to hold something of hers, something infused with her energy. I reached for her favorite blanket, the one she had carried everywhere— from the car to the couch to the foot of my bed. It still smelled faintly of her.

The woman told me she would close her eyes and take a moment to tune in. I heard her sigh, her breathing slow on the other end of the line. Then, a pause. As if she were reaching for something beyond what either of us could see, but both of us could somehow feel.

"She's trying to come through," the woman said finally, "but your grief is standing in the way. It's making it hard for her to reach you. She's nearby, just waiting for the space to open."

My eyes filled instantly.

"She's been with you longer than you know," she continued softly. "Since you were very young. Long before you ever met her in this life. She used to lay at the end of your bed—not in body, but in spirit. Nestled at your feet. Guarding and protecting you."

I could hardly believe it. All those nights I spent terrified in my childhood bedroom, convinced I was alone in the dark. Grace was there.

"She returned later in this life," the woman went on, her voice barely above a whisper, "as a dog—because she knew it was the only way you could fully receive her. She came to teach you about love, trust, surrender, and what it means to walk a sacred path."

Before we ended the call, the woman's voice shifted, and I could hear the smile in her voice—warm, almost maternal.

"Do you know much about numerology?" she asked gently.

"Very little," I admitted.

"Then this may not surprise you," she said, a hint of amusement woven into her words.

She explained that Grace had been born on 3/11—a number tied to spiritual awakening, intuition, and divine alignment. It carries the energy of soul leadership and higher purpose, of walking with conviction and inner knowing. It speaks to answering the call to uplift others through love, presence, and unwavering truth.

"She didn't come into this world by accident," the woman said. "She arrived as a guide."

Then her voice deepened, bearing a kind of timeless wisdom.
"And she passed on 1/11."

1/11—the number of new beginnings. Of individuality, transformation, and life mastery. A triple one: not just a date, but a threshold. A sign that one chapter had closed and another was ready to begin, not just for Grace, but for me.

"She left," the woman said, "exactly when she was meant to. She came to complete something with you, and when it was done, she passed the torch, not through words, but through energy, timing, and truth."

It was never just a death.
It was a handoff.
A sacred release.

She was born with her purpose already written in her spirit.
And she left as a teacher of light.

A PLACE TO BEGIN AGAIN

After Grace died, something in me changed. It wasn't only grief, though the pain of her loss lived deep in my chest. It was a breaking open, a gentle clarity that revealed what mattered most, both what I wanted to build and how I wanted to live.

I kept moving, step by step, growing my work, deepening the offerings Grace had inspired. She was no longer by my side, but her spirit lingered—in the trees, the air, the quiet in between moments—guiding me forward.

And then came the pull toward something new.
It wasn't just the next chapter, but an entirely new landscape of life.

I craved stillness, not as an escape, but as a foundation. I wanted land, a place to breathe, reflect, and plant roots. A home not just for myself, but for something more meaningful, where people could gather, exhale, and return to what is real. A retreat in the wilderness. A refuge for healing, far from the rush of everyday life. A place where the weight of the world could lift, and what had been forgotten could come back into view.

Eventually, I found it. Tucked in the heart of Colorado, cradled by ponderosa pines and nourished by snow-fed streams. The moment I stepped onto the land, something in me relaxed. Elk moved slowly through the meadow, a fox slipped like a shadow through the brush, and the mountains rose around me like guardians whispering, *You made it. Welcome home.*

Here, Grace could finally rest, her ashes returned to the same earth we once wandered together. Her spirit roaming untethered, dancing on the wind, drinking from mountain streams, curling up in starlight at the meadow's edge.

The land asked something of me. It wanted tending and devotion. So I began to shape it into a living sanctuary. I walked its edges daily, learning its rhythm. I cleared brush, hauled rocks, trimmed trees, and followed the direction of the light.

Inside, I stripped the house to its bones and rebuilt it with intention. Reclaimed barn wood beams, warm textures, and open space. The kitchen at the heart: a long wooden island with a stone top for gathering and nourishment. Nights of shared meals, deep conversation, firelight, laughter, and gratitude flowing long after the plates were cleared.

Outside, a wide deck stretched toward the trees and mountains—space for yoga, sacred circles, or quiet mornings with coffee and hummingbirds. I pictured it alive with people, barefoot and open-hearted, breathing together beneath the sky, pausing to look up at the stars, wrapped in moonlit wonder.

And in its wild embrace, I could feel Grace everywhere.

FOR MY MOTHER

I couldn't finish this book without offering my deepest gratitude to my mother. Without her, none of this would have been possible.

Our relationship was complicated, marked by misunderstandings, distance, and the kind of hurt that only happens when love runs deep. For years, we struggled to find each other across the gaps molded by pain and unmet needs. But we kept trying. We kept showing up.

Over time, through tearful conversations, honest reckonings, and the willingness to sit in our truth, we began to repair what had been broken. Piece by piece, we found our way back. Not by pretending the past hadn't happened, but by choosing to love each other through it.

She became my greatest cheerleader, the one who stood behind every dream, no matter how wild. Whether I was walking across the country, closing my therapy practice, speaking on stage, or starting something new, she never questioned the pull of my heart. She believed in me when I didn't. And when I lost sight of who I was, she gently reminded me.

She cheered for my success.
She fought for my joy.
She carried the vision with me, even when it was only a seed.

Before she passed, she visited my land. She stood on the soil that would become my home, looked out at the mountains, and breathed in the pines. She sensed what was unfolding there—a retreat, a sanctuary, a dream taking root. More than that, she saw the lives already being touched by the work born of my journey. She understood that it mattered. That it was making a difference.

I'm so grateful she got to see it.
To feel it.
To know.

She supported me when Grace died, loving me through it without trying to change what couldn't be undone. And when it was her time to go, I did the same for her.

It was in her Florida condo, the place she loved most—bright, breezy, filled with memories. Friends who had become like family came with food, stories, and tributes that made us laugh. We moved her hospital bed to the sunporch so she could look out at the water she loved. The room was lined with tall windows and wicker chairs, the cushions sun-faded, the sills scattered with sea glass and shells she had collected. Candles flickered, hymns played softly and waves rolled in the distance, rhythmic and soothing.

I sat beside her, held her hand, and told her how much I loved her. I thanked her for her strength, her love, our daily phone calls—the way we sipped tea and traded stories, even when miles apart. Those moments had meant more to me than she ever knew.

And then, from the deepest part of my heart, I asked her to visit me when she was gone. To let me know she was still near.

Moments later, a hawk appeared on the windowsill. It stood just feet away—calm, watchful, its eyes unblinking. Then it let out a piercing cry that rippled through my body before lifting off and soaring into the sky.

Hawks are often seen as messengers of the spirit world. With their sharp vision and ability to soar high above the earth, they're believed to bridge the human and the divine. When one appears at the time of a passing, it's said to signal that the soul is being guided safely into the next realm.

I didn't question it.
It was a message.
She had heard me.

Her death gave me an unexpected gift—a lesson in trust, faith, and surrender. Though much of her life had been lived in fear, she let go with peace. Her eyes softened, her energy lightened, and she radiated joy, as if she knew exactly where she was going. Witnessing that changed me. I realized that when we truly release control, we don't fall into emptiness, we return to what is most real, most holy.

That shift changes not only how we face death, but how we live.

In many ways, both she and Grace are still with me, encouraging me from the other side. I feel them often: in the silence, in the light, and in the words that arrive when I don't know what to write but somehow write anyway.

Just days before she passed, my mother looked at me with clear eyes and said,

Epilogue

"Promise me you'll finish the book. Promise me you'll share your story."

I promised. And here I am—pages later, heart laid bare, story told.

I wish she were here to hold it in her hands. To underline the parts that made her proud. But even though she can't read these words in this world, I know she's read every single one. I felt her with me the entire way, her voice, strength, and love woven into every line.

This book carries my story.
But it also carries hers.
And Grace's.

It is our legacy, born of love, shaped by loss, held together by devotion. A legacy of courage and healing.

And this—this is for them.
And for every soul who finds themselves in these pages.

May this remind you that you are not alone. That you matter.
Let it spark the courage to walk your own wild path, to soften toward the parts still healing, and to return to something greater, older, and wiser than fear.
May it guide you back to yourself. And when you forget, let it call you home—again and again—to your unwavering truth and freedom.

WRITTEN IN THE WILDERNESS

When I first began writing this book, I thought I was speaking about the wilderness. I imagined myself as a guide, reaching out from solid ground, offering wisdom from the trail. I thought I had made it through, and now I could tell the story from the other side.

But then the writing became its own wilderness walk. A whole new journey. There were obstacles I didn't anticipate, moments that tested my resolve, and days I wanted to give up. I lost my way more than once.

What I thought would be a recounting of the past became a living initiation, asking me to walk back through the fire I believed I had already survived. This book didn't come from the safety of arrival. It came from the messy middle.

The wilderness isn't something you pass through once.
You return to it each time you're ready to grow into the next version of yourself.

What I've come to realize is this:
I am not speaking about the wilderness.
I am speaking from within it.
I am still in it—being shaped, undone, and remade by it.
This isn't a story I've already lived.
It's one I am still living.

It's no coincidence I lost the first hundred pages of this book to a water spill on my computer. That version was still trying to teach from the outside, rather than surrender to the truth rising from within. It needed to be washed away so something truer could emerge.

For much of my life, I held tightly to image. I curated how I was seen, what I shared, what I hid, and how I moved through the world. That control wasn't ego; it was survival. It kept me safe when vulnerability felt dangerous, when being real felt like a risk I couldn't afford.

But this book... it's not a message.
It's a living thing.
I am the writer and the reader.

I am the story.
And I am still being written.

So I release my grip. I let go of how this lands, how it's interpreted, and how it's received. That's no longer mine to hold.

What I know now is this:
Everyone meets the wilderness in their own way.
Your path will not look like mine, and that's not only okay, it's just as it should be.
There is no one trail through the wild.
There is only your trail.
And the courage it takes to walk it.

I am grateful for what this process has revealed in me, the places that I still want to hold on to, the parts that still long to be seen, and the deeper invitation beneath it all:
To surrender.
To let discomfort teach.
To create not from control, but from transparency.

This is what it means to walk the wild path:
Not to master it, but to be mastered by it.
To let the wilderness have its way with you.
To trust that what it creates will be more honest, more whole, and more real than anything you could have planned.

ACKNOWLEDGEMENTS

There are many people who have supported me on the journey that led to this book—each one leaving an imprint on my heart and helping to inform the path I now walk with others.

To Iyanla Vanzant and the Inner Visions Institute Faculty—thank you for being a lifeline during one of the most significant transitions of my life. Your guidance, wisdom, and unrelenting truth-telling helped me uncover deeper layers of healing and integration I didn't yet know I was ready for.

To the incredible souls who supported the creation of this book—Chantelle Adams, Michelle Ireland, Lucie Ward, Gina Caruso Hussar, Leisa Peterson, Dina Varano—thank you for believing in the power of this story and helping me bring it into the world with integrity, clarity, and heart. And to Barbara Brown Taylor, whose writing reminded me that expression is not only healing, it is holy. Your words have been a lighthouse.

To the Wilderness Walk Community—each of you has walked into the unknown, bared your courageous souls, and met your shadows with fierce grace. You are the reason this work exists. Your stories live in these pages.

To the Wilderness Walk Shadow Coaches—thank you for braving the journey into your own inner wilderness so you could hold space for others. You are not just coaches—you are catalysts, leaders, and powerful ripple-makers in a world deeply in need of truth and transformation.

And finally to George Herrick—thank you for believing in the dream before it had a name. Your inspiration, encouragement, and soulful presence helped breathe life into The Wilderness Walk and everything it has come to represent. You are part of its roots.

And to my mother and Grace, who now guide me from the other side, your love continues to shape me in quiet and unseen ways. I feel your presence in the stillness, in the wilderness, and in the words that poured through me as I wrote this book. You remind me that we are never truly alone. That the bonds of love transcend time and space. That the deepest guidance often comes from beyond the veil.

This book is not mine alone. It is a weaving of every voice, every footstep, every moment of courage shared. Thank you—for walking with me.

RESOURCES + NEXT STEPS

Thank you for walking with me through these pages.

If something in this book stirred your soul, trust that it's no accident. You're being called into deeper alignment with who you are, what you came here to do, and how you want to live.

Whether you're just beginning your journey or ready to dive into the next chapter of your growth, there are many ways to continue walking this path with me:

Visit the Website
Explore offerings, journey's, programs, and free resources:
www.thewildernesswalk.com

Join Our Walkers in the Wild Community on Facebook
Walkers in the Wild is a space for courageous seekers, visionaries, and everyday trailblazers who are navigating their own wilderness within. Born from Navigating the Wilderness Within, this community is about sharing stories, reflections, and "trail markers" from the journey of personal transformation. We offer free master-classes and so much more!!
www.facebook.com/groups/338706597898773

Listen to the Podcast
Navigating the Wilderness Within—conversations and teachings to support your inner journey. Available on all major podcast platforms.

Follow on Social Media
Instagram: www.instagram.com/thewildernesswalk/
Facebook: www.facebook.com/thewildernesswalk
Youtube: www.youtube.com/@suzannehanna5

However you choose to continue, know this:
Your truth is worth listening to.
Your shadow is worth facing.
Your life is worth reclaiming.
And you don't have to walk alone.

READY TO GO DEEPER?

The words you've read are just the beginning.
What happens next is the lived experience—the integration, the embodiment, the courageous steps you take as you walk your own wilderness within.

If you feel the pull to go deeper...
To not just read these stories, but *live into your own...*
I've created a space for that.

The *Navigating the Wilderness Within* Online Companion Course is a virtual, self-guided journey—taught by me, Suzanne Hanna—that's designed to walk with you, chapter by chapter, as you uncover your truth, face your shadows, and reclaim your freedom from the inside out

Inside the course you'll receive:
Video guidance and audio teachings for each section of the book.
Guided visualizations to deepen your connection to the path.
Weekly journal prompts through the companion journal.

This course is for those ready to engage this work on a soul level. To not just explore the wilderness—but to be *transformed* by it.

To learn more and join the course visit:
www.thewildernesswalk.com/navigating-the-wilderness-within

THE NAVIGATING THE WILDERNESS WITHIN BOOK CLUB

This book was never meant to be just read—it was meant to be shared.
It's a journey, a mirror, a companion for the path you walk through fear, truth, and inner freedom. And like all meaningful journeys, it becomes even more powerful when processed with other like-minded souls.

That's why I created the Navigating the Wilderness Within Book Club—a sacred space to go deeper into the stories, reflections, and questions that have stirred something inside of you. This is more than a book club. It's a gathering of seekers, truth-tellers, and brave-hearted souls who are ready to walk the wilderness path together.

Whether you're reading on your own, hosting a group in your living room, or joining us virtually, you'll have access to:
A comprehensive Book Club Guide with discussion prompts, reflection questions, and journal practices for each chapter.
Access to live author sessions, where we explore the deeper layers behind the pages and answer your questions in real time.

This is your invitation:
To not just read—but to *engage*.
To not just reflect—but to *reclaim*.
And to be part of a living, breathing movement of transformation.

To get access to all the resources and join the book club experience, visit:
www.thewildernesswalk.com/book

We walk this path together.

Photo by Caroline White

ABOUT THE AUTHOR

Suzanne Hanna is a licensed psychotherapist, shadow work expert, and author dedicated to guiding others through profound personal transformation.

After walking 1,000 miles across the country in a radical act of healing and reclamation, she emerged with a sacred map leading back to one's most authentic self. Her own journey—through heartbreak, betrayal, loss, and rebirth—deeply informs the work she offers, which is infused with depth, devotion, and soul.

Suzanne has created a wide range of transformational retreats, programs and courses designed to support individuals on their evolutionary path—helping them face their shadows, reclaim their inner power, and live in alignment with their truth.

Learn more about her work at thewildernesswalk.com.

Soul Spark
—PUBLISHING—

Ready to share your story with the world?

If something in this book made you pause—that quiet moment of *"I could tell my story too"* or you heard the whisper of *"maybe it's my turn,"* take this as your sign to begin.

At Soul Spark Publishing, we believe stories shape the way we understand ourselves and each other. Yours is no exception—and it deserves to be guided with expertise, intention, and a whole lot of heart.

Whether you're drawn to write a memoir, capture a legacy, or shape your lived experience into story-first nonfiction, we'll walk beside you every step of the way.

Our collaborative publishing journey is intentionally small, deeply personal, and grounded in one simple truth: books can change lives—starting with the author's.
If that feels like your next chapter, we'd love to help you begin.

soulsparkpublishing.com
Your story is worthy. Let's bring it to life..

www.ingramcontent.com/pod-product-compliance
Lightning Source LLC
Chambersburg PA
CBHW021221130626
46554CB00004B/1310